TETON WILDLIFE

Trumpeter swan incubating

Pine marten

Coyote

TETON WILDLIFE

Observations by a Naturalist

BY PAUL A. JOHNSGARD

Colorado Associated University Press

*Publication of this book was made possible in part by a generous grant from
the Vanetta Rickards Betts Memorial Fund.*

For a friend who loved the Tetons;
And for anyone else who will yield to their spell.

Contents

Acknowledgments

The conception of this book occurred in the summer of 1974, when I took a camping trip through the Rocky Mountains and spent about a week in Jackson Hole. It soon became apparent that the area around the Jackson Hole Biological Station would be ideal for making extended observations on nesting sandhill cranes and trumpeter swans. I was later encouraged by the station's director, Dr. Oscar Paris, to apply for research space there the following summer. As a result, I spent parts of the summers of 1975 and 1976 at the Biological Station, and I greatly appreciate the opportunities thus provided me by the station's sponsors, the University of Wyoming and the New York Zoological Society. Additionally, the great kindness shown me by Dr. Paris and all the other researchers occupying the Station during those two years helped me enormously. Although I cannot mention them all, I am especially grateful to Dr. Thomas Collins, Dr. Alita Pinter, and Dr. Margaret Altmann for their advice and help.

To an equal degree I owe a debt of gratitude to many other biologists and friends in the Jackson Hole area. Foremost among them are Mardy and Louise Murie, as well as Bob and Inger Koedt, who generously allowed me to tramp around their property at all hours, and often treated me to coffee or conversation. Likewise, Frank and Rodello Calkins invariably asked me out to their home for meals and good companionship whenever I was in their neighborhood, and they were invaluable as a source of local information. Franz Camenzind, Charles McCurdy, Morna MacLeod, and Cindy Nielsen as well as many other "locals" helped in diverse ways, while Tom Mangelsen and Paul Geraghty both made enthusiastic field companions.

It is perhaps impossible to convey adequately the beauty and lure of the Tetons to anybody who has never been there, or to match the memories of those who have. Yet, I hope that in trying to describe the lives of a few of Jackson Hole's animals the reader may gain some sense of the beauty and complexity of their intertwined lives, and thus better appreciate the need for preserving such areas and keeping them inviolate from "development." In a sense, the greatest obligation that one who is able to do research in a national park or national wildlife refuge must recognize is the debt of admiration for the foresighted people who had the courage and strength to set aside these areas in perpetuity for their enjoyment by everyone.

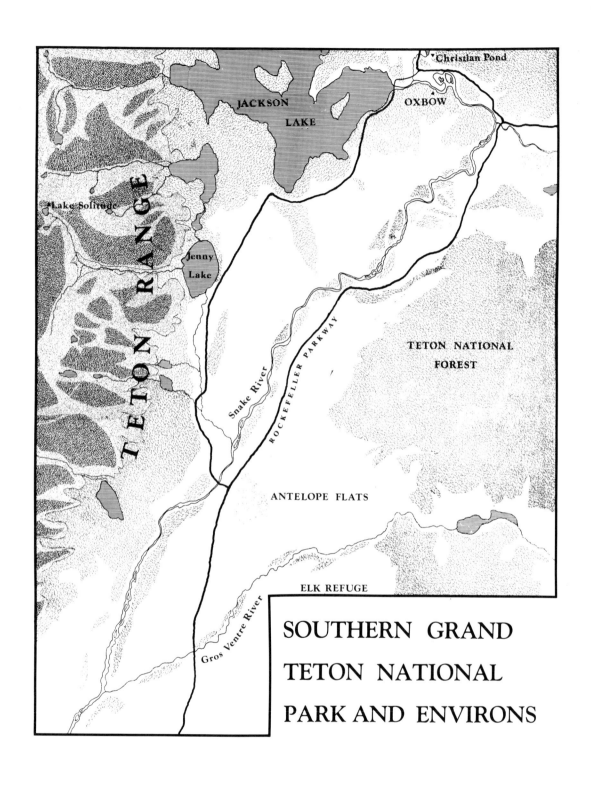

Christian Pond

JACKSON LAKE

OXBOW

TETON RANGE

Lake Solitude

Jenny Lake

Snake River

ROCKEFELLER PARKWAY

TETON NATIONAL FOREST

ANTELOPE FLATS

ELK REFUGE

Gros Ventre River

SOUTHERN GRAND
TETON NATIONAL
PARK AND ENVIRONS

1. INTRODUCTION

 The wrinkled surface of northwestern Wyoming and adjacent Idaho is a complex myriad of mountainous uplifts and basins, of varied ages and origins. In a somewhat fanciful way it resembles the imprint of a raccoon's right forefoot which, having been pressed into sticky clay, was withdrawn to form a series of ridges and peaks that subsequently solidified.

The Yellowstone and Absaroka Plateau of northwestern Wyoming represents the pawprint. Volcanic action about 30 million years ago spread ash and volcanic debris over thousands of square miles of this land's surface, and the present-day geysers, hot springs and other thermal phenomena are evidence of the area's continuing volcanic activity.

The Bridger Plateau extends southeastwardly like a narrow forefinger as the Owl Creek and Bridger Mountains, which eventually meet the "thumbprint" of the Bighorn Mountains. Between them the Bighorn River flows northward through the Bighorn Basin to join the Missouri River. To the south of the Owl Creek and Bridger Mountains is the Wind River Basin, where the Shoshone and Arapahoe Indians now live, and where the great Shoshone chief Washakie lies buried on the parched and shrub-covered hillside.

The middle "finger" of the imprint is made by the Wind River Range, the longest and highest of the Wyoming ranges. Along its crest runs the Continental Divide, and over such passes as Union Pass and South Pass

I

came the earliest explorers, mountain men, and finally emigrants on their way west. At its western base is the Green River Basin, whose waters drain into the Colorado River, and whose sedimentary rocks bear the fossil imprints of Eocene fish, reptiles, birds and mammals from 50 million years ago.

The fourth "finger" is formed basally by the jagged upthrust of the Teton Range, and farther south by the more gently folded ridges of the Wyoming and Salt River ranges, which nearly parallel the Wyoming-Idaho border. A minor range, the Gros Ventre, angles off to the east of the Tetons toward the Wind River Range.

Finally, protruding at nearly right angles westward from the Tetons and associated mountains, is the fifth "finger." This is the Centennial Range of the Idaho-Montana border, along which the Continental Divide continues westwardly.

Of all these mountain groups, much the most recent is the Teton Range, whose dramatic eastern face was exposed less than 10 million years ago by a fault in the earth's crust, where the mountains were tilted upwards and the adjoining valley floor of Jackson Hole dropped downward in a relatively rapid series of earthquake tremors. The Tetons are thus among the youngest and most spectacular of all the Rocky Mountain ranges, with their peaks and ridges having been subsequently eroded and sculptured by a variety of glacial processes, especially by ice.

As the eastern escarpment of the Tetons rose and the floor of Jackson Hole dropped, rock strata that were deposited over long periods of geologic time came into view. Indeed, the slopes of the range thus exposed to view provide a sequence of rock layers representing more than half of the earth's geologic history. The most ancient of these strata are banded Precambrian layers more than 2.5 billion years old, some of the oldest exposed rocks on the North American continent. Above these archaic rocks are sedimentary deposits less than a billion years old which formed from materials deposited along the margins of Paleozoic seas that then inundated the area. On the northern slopes of the Tetons and adjacent Gros Ventre Mountains the reddish sandstones, blue-gray limestones, gray dolomites, and black and green shales lie stacked on top of one another where layer after layer of deposits were added to older strata below, interring with them the remains of Paleozoic animals such as trilobites and brachiopods.

As the Paleozoic seas gave way to those of the Mesozoic era about 200 million years ago, soft reddish, iron-rich sediments as much as 1,000 feet thick were laid down, and now may be seen on the northern flanks of the Gros Ventre Mountains. These more brightly colored rocks were subsequently covered by a much thicker layer of dull-hued silt, sand and clay toward the end of the Mesozoic era, leaving a flat and featureless floodplain as the Mesozoic sea finally retreated eastwardly. At the very end of Mesozoic times, about 65 million years ago, mountain-building in the area began as the Wind River Range gradually lifted upwards.

During the last 65 million years, the Cenozoic era, massive mountain-building occured in North America, and most of the modern groups of birds and mammals evolved. Uplifts in several areas of what is now Wyoming produced the first of the Rocky Mountains, and erosion simultaneously began to bury the adjacent basins. One fault along the western slope of the Tetons produced the earliest uplifting and exposure of Precambrian rocks to erosive processes; a second and much later uplift along the Teton fault east of the range was to determine the eventual formation of the Teton Range.

A new geologic element was added to the massive and generally widespread forces of mountain-building and basin-filling about 50 million years ago, when volcanic eruptions from the Yellowstone and Absaroka region dropped enormous amounts of lava and other volcanic debris on the adjacent landscape. Several thousand feet of these materials blanketed eastern Jackson Hole and covered some of the older eroded mountains. Later, volcanic activity extended to the Tetons. About this time, 8 to 10 million years ago, a large freshwater lake previously formed at the eastern base of the emerging Teton range gradually began to dry up or be filled with volcanic sediments. Analysis of these lake sediments indicate that the area was inhabited by a variety of marsh and aquatic animals, such as snails, frogs and beavers, and with adjacent forests of fir, spruce, pine and associated plants.

Mount Teewinot in late spring.

Also about this time, movement along the Teton fault at the base of the mountains' eastern face initiated the tremendous uplift of the Tetons. Displacement of nearly 30,000 feet eventually occurred, lifting the eastern slope of the Tetons high over Jackson Hole, and exposing their craggy surfaces to erosion by wind, water and ice. As the floor of Jackson Hole subsided, it was covered twice by lakes for long periods of time. The first lake was eventually drained by additional warping and faulting of the earth's crust. The second lake persisted until less than a million years ago, or perhaps almost until the initial glaciation that scoured the area and sculpted the Tetons into their present-day form.

The first and most widespread of these glaciations probably occurred about 200,000 years ago. Its ice centers were in the Beartooth Mountains northeast of Yellowstone National Park and in the Absaroka and Wind River Ranges. Ice sheets up to 2,000 feet deep streamed slowly southward past the eastern face of the Tetons, through Jackson Hole and the constricted canyon of the present-day Snake River, and then westward into Idaho. Their meltwaters ultimately drained into the Pacific Ocean via the Columbia River. The second and considerably smaller glaciation may have occurred about 50,000 years ago, when glaciers from the Tetons and the Absaroka ranges merged and spread onto the floor of Jackson Hole. The third and smallest glaciation, perhaps as recently as 9,000 years ago, covered much of what is now Jackson Lake with ice. As it receded, its meltwaters cut through its terminal moraine to form the present channel of the Snake River. Further, Cow Lake, Hedrick's Pond, Christian Pond and the "Potholes" near the mouth of modern Jackson Lake formed in depressions in the outwash moraine left by the receding glacier. By this time, Jackson Hole was apparently already occupied by aborigines, and these ponds and lakes doubtless provided excellent hunting grounds.

Evidence of prehistoric use of the Tetons by humans is still very limited, but an inundated campsite at the north end of Jackson Lake suggests that Paleo-Indians may have been using the area as early as 10 or 11 thousand years ago, and quite certainly were by 5,000 to 7,000 B.C. They were probably culturally related to the Plains Indians who depended on

5

hunting a prehistoric species of bison. This bison eventually became extinct during a warm and dry period that persisted until about 2,500 B.C. Thereafter, the modern species of bison appeared on the Great Plains. With it came a culture of Plains Indians that exploited these herds. By about 500 A.D. these Indians shifted from the spear to the bow and arrow as their primary weapon. This transition marks the start of the Late Prehistoric Period. Traps for bison and antelope, probably used by Shoshone Indians, have been found south of the Tetons. The Shoshones apparently made regular visits to the Tetons and Yellowstone region to obtain glass-like obsidian, volcanic stone for weapons points and tools.

The first white man to see the area was probably John Colter, who came through Union Pass in 1807 and explored the Yellowstone plateau in 1808. His incredible stories of the area stimulated the arrival of explorers, trappers, hunters and finally settlers. Jackson Hole (originally Jackson's Hole, meaning valley) was named after David Jackson, an early trapper. French-speaking trappers call the high, central peaks *Les Trois Tetons*, or "the three breasts." This was, perhaps, a less apt name than that of the Shoshones, who had hunted there for generations and referred to them as *Teewinot*, or "many pinnacles."

2. THE VALLEY OF THE GROS VENTRE

The highest point in the Wind River Range and indeed all of Wyoming is Gannett Peak, which towers nearly 14,000 feet above sea level. About 25 miles north is Three Waters Mountain, an enormous massif whose summits form several miles of the Continental Divide. Its eastern slopes drain into creeks that flow into such famous rivers as the Wind, the Bighorn, the Yellowstone, the Missouri, and the Mississippi. Water draining off its broad, inclined southwestern flanks forms the headwaters of the Green River, which merges with the Colorado, and finally empties into the Gulf of California. Water from its northwestern slope flows to yet a third destination, the Gros Ventre River. This river, named for the tribe of Atsina Blackfeet that periodically moved through the area from their Montana home, flows into the Snake River. The Snake, in turn, joins the Columbia River, and the Columbia River feeds the Pacific Ocean.

The treeless alpine zone of these mountains is snow-covered for all but a month or two in late summer, when a meadow-like carpet of grasses, sedges, and more colorful flowering plants suddenly emerge, and provide summer foods for bighorn sheep, elk and yellow-bellied marmots. Here, amidst glinting talus slopes, pikas cut and cure supplies of grass during summer in preparation for winter, and black rosy finches nest in the rock crevices.

Timberline on the northwestern slope of Three Waters Mountain exceeds 10,000 feet in favored situations, where ancient whitebark pines form the uppermost battlements of the forest. Their stunted and twisted trunks survive for several centuries, gaining sustenance during brief summers, and standing resolute against winter winds. Here too, snow melt from the alpine tundra above forms small ponds in depressions, overflows, and drains into Fish Creek, then the Gros Ventre.

As the youthful Fish Creek dances down the mountainside, it passes the timberline stands of whitebark pines, and soon enters the highest zone of true forest, the Engelmann spruce-subalpine fir community. Although snow persists well into June at these high elevations, the cool forests attract elk and mule deer escaping summer's heat and flies, and they ring then with songs of hermit and Swainson's thrushes, mountain chickadees, western tanagers, and Oregon juncos. The less conspicuous high-pitched notes of golden-crowned and ruby-crowned kinglets are also present, like vocal zephyrs in the needlelike foliage, and the junco-like chant of the yellow-rumped warbler, while Clark's nutcrackers periodically scream from the taller trees.

Blue grouse.

8

As Fish Creek flows to join the Gros Ventre, the spruces and subalpine firs gradually give way to Douglas fir and, where there has been a history of fire, lodgepole pine. Wildlife use of Douglas fir forests is much the same as for the higher spruce-fir zone; here snowshoe hares and red squirrels are common, and are preyed upon by pine martens and lynxes, while blue grouse hoot in late spring from the forest openings. The lodgepole pine forests are essentially even-aged stands of trees less than a century old, which were initiated by forest fires that stimulated seed-dropping by these fire-adapted trees. Their crowded and monotonously similar structure supports but a limited variety of birds and mammals; chipping sparrows and dark-eyed juncos forage on the forest floor, mountain chickadees search out insects in dark crevices, and yellow-rumped warblers and western tanagers catch insects amid the canopy foliage. The most conspicuous avian residents are the gray jays and Clark's nutcrackers, which with pine siskins subsist on seeds and other food gathered in the foliage and elsewhere.

As the river makes its way down the Gros Ventre Canyon, it is twice temporarily impounded in small lakes; Upper Slide Lake and Lower Slide Lake. Lower Slide Lake was produced by a massive landslide in 1925 that sent millions of tons of soil and rock down the mountainside, totally damming the river. Later, the impounded waters burst through the slide debris and flooded the downstream village of Kelly, with the loss of 80 homes and six lives. As the Gros Ventre flows out of Lower Slide Lake and past the nearly deserted village of Kelly, it emerges onto the floor of Jackson Hole, and leaves the coniferous forest behind.

The lower fringes of the coniferous forest are often marked by aspen groves, which grow on hillsides too dry to support coniferous forests, and on level sites adjacent to meadows and swamps. The aspen community is extremely important to wildlife; its buds and twigs are browsed by elk, moose and deer, and by ruffed grouse in winter. Its bark is the primary food of the beaver. Although the hillside stands of aspen are relatively low in both plant and bird diversity, flatland stands have a remarkably rich array of birds. Feeding on the ground are common flickers, moun-

9

tain bluebirds, American robins, Lincoln's sparrows, and white-crowned sparrows. Yellow-bellied sapsuckers drill regularly spaced holes in aspen bark to draw sap, calliope hummingbirds seek out nectar-containing flowers, and a variety of insect-eating birds such as yellow and MacGillivray's warblers, black-headed grosbeaks, and house wrens harvest the abundant insects.

Soon the Gros Ventre begins to assume a new character; its streambed becomes broader and more wandering as it cuts new channels and forms islands and oxbows in the soft glacial till of Jackson Hole. Stands of willows and cottonwoods grow along its banks, and willow and sedge thickets extend outward in the water-rich soils. Beyond the effects of the river, sagebrush covers the low hills. The river's edge is the National Elk Refuge's northern boundary as well as the southern boundary of Grand Teton National Park.

The cottonwoods and willows along the Gros Ventre are the habitats of water shrews, mink and meadow voles, and support a dense summer population of yellow warblers, MacGillivray's warblers, common yellowthroats and song sparrows. White-crowned sparrows sing from low shrubbery, and common snipes probe the moist soil. Lincoln's sparrows, fox sparrows, and American robins work through the underbrush, while wood pewees and willow flycatchers use the tallest willows and cottonwoods as convenient perches from which they fly out to hawk passing insects.

Where the soil becomes too dry to support a streamside forest, sagebrush dominates and lends tones of silvery green to the landscape of Jackson Hole. It is the winter habitat of elk and bison, and throughout the year white-tailed jackrabbits, coyotes and badgers are present. Sage grouse, vesper sparrows and Brewer's sparrows are characteristic breeding birds of the sagebrush community, and both red-tailed and Swainson's hawks glide above the sagebrush flats in search of such rodents as the ubiquitous Uinta ground squirrels. As the mountains become snow-free in spring, small herds of pronghorn move down the valley of the Gros Ventre River to forage on the sagebrush-dominated Antelope Flats.

A small herd of bison inhabits Jackson Hole throughout the year.

The slopes and buttes of the National Elk Refuge are nearly devoid of trees, but runoff from the Gros Ventre Range to the south, and from springs at the foot of the mountains spreads into marshes along Flat Creek. From the time that deep snow drives elk out of their high mountain meadows, usually in November or December, until late March or April, the National Elk Refuge is the traditional winter home of about 8,000 elk.

The elk of the Yellowstone and Grand Teton area consists of several herds. The largest two are a northern herd that summers through most of Yellowstone National Park and winters in the Yellowstone River Valley, and a southern or Jackson Hole herd that summers in the highlands around Jackson Hole and the headwaters of the Snake River in southern Yellowstone Park, and winters in Jackson Hole and southward. The National Elk Refuge was established in 1912 to protect and provide emergency winter food for these wintering animals, which, since settlement of Jackson Hole, had been increasingly dependent on foraging on private lands to survive. From its original size of less than 2,000 acres, the refuge gradually grew to nearly 24,000 acres by 1935.

By the time the elk arrive on their wintering grounds, the mating period is over, and the elk are in mixed-sex groups in which females strongly predominate. This partly reflects the tendency for adult males to winter on high, wind-swept ridges, and partly the unbalanced sex ratio typical of polygamous mammals.

By mid-winter the elk are strongly concentrated on the refuge feeding grounds, and extensive supplementary feeding of alfalfa pellets is usually required to ensure their survival. Sharing the winter range with the elk is a flock of trumpeter swans, which forage in the relatively warm and unfrozen waters of Flat Creek. The swans are attracted there from both Yellowstone and Grand Teton parks. Coyotes patrol the herds daily, waiting for crippled or sick elk to succumb, and quickly devouring carcasses as they become available. February and March are the most critical months for elk not wintering on the refuge and other State of Wyoming feed grounds. Although the worst winter weather may be over, supplies

"As the elk begin to leave the refuge, so too do most of the wintering trumpeter swans."

of the more accessible and edible plants are gone, and the elk may turn to aspen bark, be forced to dig through heavy snow to uncover sedges, willows and rabbitbrush, or may even resort to eating pine and fir needles. By mid-February, deaths from a bacterial infection of the mouth may become numerous, and ravens, bald eagles, and coyotes briefly share the feast provided by dying elk. In late February males begin to lose their antlers. By mid-March they have nearly all been dropped and new ones have begun to grow. By then, too, females are six months pregnant, or only two months from calving. The first thawing of snow cover in March thus comes none too soon, and renews life for the elk.

As the snow cover begins to retreat up the hillsides of the Elk Refuge in late March and early April, the large concentrated herds of elk begin to break up into smaller groups, which move into side valleys and lower slopes. Slowly, the first elk begin to leave the refuge. About half are mature, and ten to twenty percent are bulls. Roughly three-fourths of the adult females are pregnant and will give birth by late May or early June. Typically, the first elk to leave for the summer range are individual or small groups of old bulls. Next are groups of yearlings, two-year-old cows,

13

and "dry" cows. Lastly come the pregnant cows, moving slowly and destined to give birth before they reach their summer range. The northward-moving elk are in groups of a few to as many as 40 or 50, typically led by an experienced mature female. She chooses the route and the time and place of crossing rivers, with the other elk following dutifully.

As the elk begin to leave the refuge, so too do most of the wintering trumpeter swans. They disperse in pairs and family groups to more northerly waters that are slowly becoming ice-free. Wintering Canada geese on Flat Creek also become restless, as do Barrow's goldeneyes and mallards. By late March some of the Canada geese will have moved up the Snake River toward Jackson Lake and northward into the river's headwaters near Yellowstone Park, while others arrive on the Elk River from more southerly wintering grounds. As they work their way up the Snake River, they fly over occasional groups of common mergansers fishing in the river, and past a pair of bald eagles, which by late March are already renovating their last-year's nest to receive a new clutch of eggs.

By early April the Elk Refuge suddenly seems unusually full of potential; the swans and Canada geese are trumpeting their departure northward, the bull elk are milling about and beginning to drift off the refuge into the wooded hills, and the sounds of courting goldeneyes enliven Flat Creek. Small flocks of green-winged teal, pintails, and wigeon appear on Flat Creek, and male sage grouse gather on snow-free ridges to begin their territorial displays. Up the valley of the Snake River comes the first distant bugles of migrating sandhill cranes, and the sagebrush flats are starting to green up with the earliest of the spring grasses and flowers.

3. THE SAGEBRUSH SEA

 Like a silvery green sheet, the sagebrush flats of Jackson Hole spread almost uninterrupted from the base of the Gros Ventre Mountains to the Teton Range, providing unspoken testimony to the survival value of patience and fortitude in a semi-arid environment. The species of sagebrush dominating these flats is part of a vegetational type that evolved and spread widely throughout the intermountain west during the uplift of the Rocky Mountains more than 20 million years ago. Only a few other species of shrubs, mainly rabbit-brush and some other sagebrush species, manage to compete effectively with big sagebrush for the limited supply of water and associated nutrients on these flats. At their edges, however, the battle for vegetational dominance is constantly waged among sagebrush, aspen, and lodgepole pine. Where the land rises but a few hundred feet above the flats, stands of lodgepole pine form the primary shoreline of the sagebrush sea, while on arid hillsides occasional islands of aspens emerge out of the sagebrush flats like becalmed and abandoned ships in a windless ocean. But the sagebrush flats are anything but lifeless.

One early spring day a pair of coyotes began digging a den on a sage-scented hillside. The den was scarcely visible on the sun-warmed southern slope facing the Snake River valley. The female began to dig it on a warm day in March, about a month after becoming pregnant. The entrance, well-concealed by low sagebrush, was less than a foot wide and about two feet high. It extended back several feet to a widened area about three feet in diameter, above which an abandoned ground squirrel hole provided a built-in ventilation shaft to the surface. It was but one of several burrows that the pair of coyotes had throughout their extensive home range. Some they used for midday retreats on hot summer days. Several were merely abandoned badger holes.

As the late April sun began to stir spring flowers to life, the female came to full term, and lay in the den patiently awaiting birth of her litter. She had already removed the hair from her belly, exposing her milk-swollen nipples. Her mate remained nearby, only periodically leaving her to check the now mostly barren skeletons of winter-killed elk or to return with a meadow vole, a small rodent that is the bread-and-butter component of a coyote's diet in Jackson Hole. The two-year-old female, pregnant for the first time, had become progressively less tolerant of her mate's presence in the den during the past few days. Finally, as he returned from one of his mouse-hunting forays, he seemed surprised that, instead of being greeted by his mate's usual muzzle-grasping greeting, she lifted her ears, retracted her lips, and uttered a throaty growl. The confused male quickly retracted his ears and backed out of the den, unaware that the first of his six offspring was about to be born.

As the half-pound pups emerged, they were carefully cleaned by the mother with her tongue, exposing a dark, tawny brown fur, with slightly darker areas on their ears, faces, backs and tails. Their eyes were shut tightly, their rounded ears lay flat against the head, and a short length of umbilical cord extended from their bodies. As the female cleaned each pup, she started by licking around the head, the first part of the pup to emerge. Aided by their mother's licking and muzzle movements, the newborn pups slowly worked their way along her belly and firmly attached themselves to her nipples. They formed a row of brown, furry objects; their heads gently resting on the mother's belly and their bodies in contact with one another for the entire length.

Adult coyote.

Life in the den for the next two weeks consisted of little more than alternating sleeping and nursing, with occasional excited squeaks from a pup when it lost physical contact with its mother or the other youngsters. After ten days, the pups' pink footpads had turned black, and their umbilical wounds had healed completely. Their teeth were nearly ready to break through the gums, and the inside corners of the pups' eyes were beginning to part. A few days later their eyes were fully open, and their ears were starting to become functional, making them aware for the first time that outside their den existed a world they would soon be eager to explore.

Within a few days of opening their eyes, the pups began to practice walking, and by the time they were three weeks old, all six were actively investigating the limits of their den. Throughout this vulnerable period the male remained very close to the den, sometimes approaching its entrance, but usually remaining as inconspicuous as possible while guarding it. Whenever a pup began to stray too close to the den's entrance a whine or squeak from the mother was enough to turn it back. At three weeks of age, the pups' canine teeth emerged, and when they approached the female to nurse, her behavior changed from acceptance to a low growl and avoidance. By then her belly and nipples were raw and sometimes bleeding from the nearly constant biting and scratching of her active litter. At times, she ran out of the den to avoid the hungry pups, and whenever they followed her the male gently picked them up by the head or body and carried them back to the safety of the den.

When the litter was some three weeks old, the female began to remain away from her den for an hour or more, leaving her mate to guard it against other coyotes while she searched the hillside for food. Soon she returned, uttering a whine that attracted the entire litter. As the pups pawed at her mouth and excitedly wagged their tails, she heaved convulsively and regurgitated several partially digested mice in front of the pups. For the next two weeks the pattern remained much the same, with both parents bringing food and almost no nursing allowed by the female. Soon the young began to make short forays away from the den's entrance,

Howling coyote.

spending their spare time in the rough-housing and play-fighting that establishes dominance relationships so important to their later social life.

As the pups approached their fourth week of age near the end of May, they divided their time between feeding and fighting with their litter mates. Fights at this stage have little of the playfulness typical of older animals with established dominance positions. Instead their fights consisted of unrestrained biting and head-shaking movements, with the bites directed toward the face, neck-scruff or body. As each pup engaged in such fights, individual differences in strength and aggressiveness became apparent, and within a few days a dominance order began to emerge. Almost immediately the most and least dominant positions became established, but the other four pups took longer to establish their relationships with one another. When a clear hierarchy had been established, their serious fighting was gradually replaced with play-fighting. This usually started with an invitation-to-play posture by one pup, which crouched on its forelegs while keeping its hindquarters elevated, or by

19

making approach and withdrawal movements. Jaw-wrestling, inhibited biting, and general body wrestling were interspersed with short chases. These bouts usually ended with the dominant pup standing victoriously above the subordinate one, who lay quietly and submissively underneath.

By the time the female completely weaned her young in May, they fed almost entirely on mice. This diet was soon supplemented by the much larger pocket gophers as these rodents became increasingly active above ground, and as the snow cover that had provided their winter protection disappeared from the bottomlands. While snow cover was still patchy, the male coyote concentrated his hunting on the snowfields, where he stealthily prowled, listening for mouse activity below. As soon as he heard or scented one, he suddenly stopped and poised for a pounce, with his ears pointed forward and his tail irrepressibly wagging. Then he would suddenly spring almost vertically upward and crash through the snow cover with his forelegs, trapping the mouse in his paws. However, as the snow cover disappeared the male spent much more time hunting for pocket gophers, since they could be easily caught by simply waiting at their tunnel entrance until they emerged.

After April had passed into memory, and the snowline rose inexorably up the foothills to the east, a small herd of pronghorn began to move down from the Gros Ventre valley, after wintering in the Green River drainage. In Jackson Hole the snow cover is too deep for them to survive without danger of starvation. Thus each spring a small band migrates west into the upper Gros Ventre drainage between Bacon and Red Bluff Ridges. By April the bucks had mostly regrown the horny sheaths of their antlers, which they had shed the previous fall after the rut. Nearly all does in the herd at least two years old were pregnant, having carried their developing young through the winter. The pronghorns travelled in one group for maximum safety from coyotes or other predators. So long as they could avoid crossing deep snow their vulnerability to predation was minimal, but in soft snow they risked becoming bogged down and unable to escape the lighter and more agile coyotes. As the pronghorn

Pronghorn adult male

finally reached the lower flatlands of the Gros Ventre Range in late May they separated into several groups and spread out over Antelope Flats.

The adult males immediately established territories. Those that had been territorial the previous year simply returned to the same areas, while newly maturing males tried to establish territories for the first time. Most of the immature males formed a separate herd that moved about the areas not defended by mature males, and a few bachelor males stayed to themselves. The does comprised the last major group, which wandered at will over the flats, but were almost always accompanied by the resident buck through whose territory they passed.

As each adult buck returned to his old territory or attempted to establish a new one, his behavior was predictable. After attaining sexual maturity, each buck attempts to establish local social dominance every summer by marking various points about the area he selects for a territory. Periodically he would stop, paw the ground, urinate, defecate, and then move on to the next marking location. Wherever a large shrub or other unusually tall plant occurred, he would sniff it, chew or bite off the tip of the plant, and rub his blackish cheek patch against it. Thus he transmitted his distinctive scent to the plant, and established an olfactory "signpost" proclaiming ownership of the area. This marking was especially frequent wherever a possible visual or olfactory contact with another buck's territory might occur.

Whenever a male actually intruded into the territory of another, the response of the resident male was immediate and unmistakable. Snorting an alarm, he would then utter a series of wheezing notes descending in volume and pitch. Often these were sufficient to cause the intruder to flee, especially if it were a yearling. Otherwise the intruder was immediately approached and threatened. Walking deliberately toward him, the resident male lowered his head, compressed his mane and rump patch, and stared directly at the intruder. If this still failed to deter him, the resident male stood broadside about five or ten yards away, or the two males would walk parallel to each other at this distance, occasionally depositing territorial markers along the way. These displays, alone or

Female pronghorn and yearling.

collectively, were usually enough to cause the intruder to leave without contesting the issue further.

By the middle of May the does approached the end of their pregnancies, and the female herd began to break up. Each pregnant female, sometimes accompanied by her yearling fawn, sought out a suitable place to give birth, usually a place where the sagebrush was at least 20 inches high and thus tall enough to hide a newborn fawn.

Such a site was selected by a two-year-old female one day in late May. Lying down in the heavy sage, she began to lick her udder and belly, occasionally standing up and walking about for short distances. Her two fawns were born less than thirty minutes apart. As soon as each was free of the mother, she licked it, thus removing the fetal membranes and perhaps also stimulating it to breathe. Almost as soon as it had been cleaned, the fawn struggled to rise, and within 30 minutes of being born was on its feet and attempting to walk. On finding its mother, each fawn sought out her udder. She responded by standing still and arching her back to allow sucking. When but a few hours old, the well-nursed fawns began to make short forays away from the mother, and soon bedded down nearly twenty yards away from her. Amazingly, except for the relatively short time spent nursing, essentially all of the newborn's time was spent out of physical contact with its mother while lying motionless on the ground. Probably this represents an anti-predator adaptation. The young fawns are easy prey for coyotes, but they rarely find fawns, and usually are not a major threat to a fawn's survival.

By the time that they were two weeks old, the fawns began to form groups, producing a nucleus of nursery herds made up of newborns and their mothers. Although fawns in these groups attempted to nurse from females other than their mothers, they were quickly rejected by being gently butted away. In these nursery groups the fawns associated almost entirely with others fawns, since their mothers leave them unattended except for short periods of nursing and grooming. By late August, male fawns started to perform pairing behavior toward their mothers, and the weaning process was well underway. Nursing gradually diminished as the

Young male pronghorn.

fall rut approached, and adult males began intensively courting the mature females.

As summer ended, the territorial males spent an increasing amount of their time trying to herd females toward the centers of their respective territories. Likewise, the mature but nonterritorial males, which previously moved about the area in groups or alone, now spent increasingly more time trying to intrude into the territories of established males. Fighting resulting from these encounters sharply increased, and by the end of September many males were limping or showing patches of missing hair where they had been badly bitten.

Male moose with antlers in velvet.

4. THE WILLOW FLATS

As a small flock of greater sandhill cranes flew north out of the Elk Refuge in late April, they gradually broke up into the four life-long pairs that had been formed several years previously. Two pairs remained on the Elk Refuge to establish territories along Flat Creek, another settled into a beaver pond on a small creek below Teton Point overlook in Grand Teton National Park, and a third pair headed for a beaver pond on lower Buffalo Fork River. The remaining pair continued north to the willow flats just below Jackson Lake dam.

This table-flat area of willow thickets and boggy grasslands is impenetrable to nearly all large mammals except moose, is rich in succulent green plants, and has adjoining areas of sagebrush where the cranes can easily forage on the roots and shoots of sprouting spring herbs. Even coyotes, which regularly hunted mice on the sagebrush flats, tended to avoid the heavy vegetation of the wet willows in favor of easier hunting grounds. But moose reveled in the combination of willow cover and shallow ponds. For several months a small group had been wintering here, eating almost nothing but willow twigs and often cropping the branches down to the snow-line. The cow moose with their nearly year-old calves wandered through the area avoiding contact with other moose, while the antlerless males often mingled in twos or threes.

The cranes, finding their last-year's nesting territory still under a foot of snow, flew daily to the sage-covered hillsides, where south-facing slopes provided snow-free ground and an abundance of spring plants. With their chisel-like bills, they dug up the enlarged roots of springbeauties, keeping a watchful eye for coyotes and periodically announcing their ownership of the entire area with their unison calling.

Their appetites temporarily quieted, the pair flew to the edge of a marshy creek, where they waded and dug up mud and decaying vegetation of the previous year. Then they methodically spread these materials over their almost uniformly gray winter plumage, slowly staining it rusty brown except for their heads and upper necks, which they could not reach. Gradually the birds came to resemble more closely the dead-plant background where their nest would soon be located.

Sandhill cranes dancing

As the pair claimed their 50-acre territory on the flats, they spent part of each day calling simultaneously, with their bills pointed skyward, their wings slightly drooped, and the decurved inner wing feathers slightly raised. Sometimes when they had finished calling one would reach down to the ground, pick up a bit of vegetation, and throw it high above its head. Then, on stiffened legs, the pair would bound into the air, spreading and thrusting their wings downward with each leap, and raising them again as they landed. With each bound they lowered their heads and necks in a kind of bowing posture as they faced each other. Often, as they leapt into the air they would turn slightly, landing at a somewhat different angle. Thus the two birds gradually revolved around a point as they danced and called exuberantly. The dance stopped as unexpectedly as it began, and the birds soon began preening sedately, as if nothing had happened.

This was the second year this pair of cranes had attempted to nest. Each was approaching five years of age. The male had been hatched near Grays Lake in eastern Idaho, and the female was one of the few cranes that had been hatched and raised in the grassy meadows of the National Elk Refuge near Jackson. The pair had met and formed a mating bond on their wintering grounds of central New Mexico two winters before, and the female had led her mate northeastward from their spring staging area near Bear Lake. They had established their first nesting territory around a small beaver pond in willows that moose had clipped nearly to the surface. But their first nesting effort had met with disaster; a raven had watched the entire nest-building proceedings, and patiently awaited its opportunity. The close guarding of the nest by both parents had effectively forced the raven to keep a safe distance away until well into the incubation period, when one day a cow moose nearly stepped on the incubating bird. With a frightened scream the crane flew from the nest. Before her mate could drive the moose away with its flailing wings and beak, the raven had quickly flown in and neatly pierced both eggs. Whether out of inexperience or otherwise, the cranes simply abandoned

29

Sandhill crane nesting in the willow flats.

their territory, and spent the rest of the summer in a remote meadow, where they molted and underwent their flightless period.

This spring the cranes had selected a nesting site close to their previous year's nest, but on a beaver lodge surrounded by water. This provided a commanding view of the adjacent flats, and was unlikely to be trodden upon by a foraging moose. At the same time, the brown-colored birds blended well with the lodge. When the incubating crane lowered its head and neck as far as possible, it resembled nothing more than an unusually large log on the top of the lodge.

During the second week of May the pair had attained undisputed ownership of the willow flats; the only other cranes in the vicinity were nesting more than a mile away on the Oxbow island. Another pair was using the sedge meadow at the northern end of Christian Pond. The three pairs were in daily vocal contact, hurling territorial threats at one another, but sometimes two of the pairs occupied neutral ground together while foraging on the sagebrush hillsides.

As the female made the few adjustments to the top of the lodge needed to make it a suitable nest, the male closely patrolled the area for signs of coyotes and moose. Every coyote seen was closely watched and followed discreetly. If one happened to approach the nest too closely it could be readily lured away with a "broken-wing act." The few pregnant cow moose that ambled through the area soon learned to avoid the vicinity of the beaver lodge after being fiercely attacked by the male crane.

Occasionally, the male would visit the nest and help with its construction. The week prior to egg-laying the pair mated almost daily, often between foraging sessions. Circling the female from behind, the male approached cautiously as the female tilted her head upwards at a forty-five degree angle, and while lowering and partially spreading her wings. He mounted her by placing his toes over the leading edges of her wings, lowering his feet so they rested on her wings, and grasped her nape with his bill. Slowly flexing his wings to maintain balance, the male quickly completed mating, then jumped forward to stand beside his mate in an arched-neck posture. Later, after the pair had preened at length, the female returned to her nest.

The female laid her first egg, a study in earth tones of brown, buff and black, on May 13; the second on May 15. By then, not only was the lodge snow-free, but the pond was entirely thawed and snow was mostly limited to the interiors of the willow clumps that lined the pond. During the time between the laying of the two eggs, the female never left the nest. As soon as the second egg was laid, the male approached the nest, moved a few twigs around with his bill, and eased the female off the nest. Thereafter the two birds took turns incubating, often for sessions of several hours,

31

with the female taking over in late afternoon to remain on the nest through the night, while the male stood guard nearby.

Within the crane's territory were also a pair of nesting common snipes, a nest each of green-winged teal and mallards, and several pair of yellow warblers and common yellowthroats. Each of these species was as closely tied to the willows as the moose and beaver. The snipes and ducks nested at the base of willow clumps, and the warblers nested in the crotches of branches. The male warblers persistently advertised their territories with singing, but the male ducks had already abandoned their mates and were gathering with others in small groups along the shore of Christian Pond. Every morning and evening was marked by the distinctive sound of winnowing snipe. High above the marsh the male performed an undulating territorial flight consisting of climbs alternating with shallow dives, while simultaneously spreading his outer tail feathers as far as possible. These narrow feathers were set into noisy vibration, which was regularly interrupted as his moving wings intercepted the airflow. After several minutes of circling the beaver pond, the snipe suddenly raised his wings nearly vertically and dropped quickly back into the marsh near the crane nest.

With the laying of her second egg, the female crane or her mate remained constantly on the nest, inconspicuously observing activities around the pond, and periodically turning their heads sideways to watch a pair of red-tailed hawks wheeling in the sky, seemingly sweeping it clean with their orderly convolutions.

On Blacktail Butte to the south, the old dirty snow gradually was replaced with the pink tones of springbeauties. Nearby, a male bald eagle kept his daily heraldic vigil near the top of a dead cottonwood, patiently staring at the rushing water below him, as if trying to find some hidden meaning to life in the swirling currents.

By early June the lifeless brown willow flats had been transformed into a brilliant green, and the rich, brown-stained plumage of the nesting cranes had become increasingly conspicuous to the ravens that made periodic inspection flights over the beaver pond. The morning din of warblers, snipes, and chorus frogs began progressively earlier, and the eastern face of Mount Moran became ever more pink with alpenglow each morning as the sun neared the northern end of its seasonal circuit.

In mid-June, 30 days after the cranes began incubating, one of the two eggs began to click and vibrate, as a tiny excavation appeared at its larger end. The female sat even more closely, only occasionally standing up to look at the pipping egg, and sometimes to move it gently with her bill. Then she would settle back down, aligning the eggs so they rested on either side of her breastbone parallel to each other. After 24 hours of pipping, the first chick finally kicked free of its shell, and lay cold and wet in the nest. Its golden brown down soon dried, and the chick was quickly transformed into an enchanting fluff of newly minted gold, with a pale-tipped pink bill and sprawling, pinkish-blue legs and feet that seemed three times too large for its body. The female reached down and slowly nudged the chick with her bill until it moved to the warm pocket of safety between her flanks and her folded wings, and then settled back down to await the hatching of her second egg, which was just starting to pip. Within a few hours the chick peeked out from the bend of its mother's wing and tried to climb up on her back. By then the mother had crushed the remains of the hatched egg. After eating most of it herself, she held tiny fragments before the chick's bill. Perhaps responding to its whiteness, the chick opened its bill and began to nibble at the bits of shell.

Soon it was scrambling actively over the mother's back, and as the male climbed back on to the nest to take over tending the remaining egg, the chick followed its mother as she slowly moved away from the nest. Floating lightly on the water, the chick quickly paddled behind its wading mother, occasionally stopping to peck at a bit of floating debris, or a swimming insect. Soon it tired and moved back to the nest where it snuggled close against its father's underwing. When its mother finished foraging, she returned to the nest, and pushed her mate aside. Through the night the female tended her chick and the pipping egg, and by the following dawn the second chick was also free of its shell and drying in the nest beside its older sibling.

By noon the second chick was dry and actively wriggling around in the nest with its mother. The other chick tagged closely behind the adult male, which ever more impatiently began to stray farther from the nest toward heavier cover provided by aspens and cottonwoods. Soon the female, in response to the repeated soft calls of her mate, stood up in the nest, nudged the chick with her bill, and called softly. Responding with a peeping note, the youngster stood on its gangling legs and followed her as she gradually moved toward her mate. Then, with the male in the lead, the older chick at his heels, the female next in line, and the young chick beside her, the family slowly moved away from the nest for the last time. In its cup the crumpled remains of the second eggshell were the only evidence of the drama that had so recently unfolded.

By the time they were only a week old, the two crane chicks had grown remarkably and could realistically be called colts. The color of golden palominos, the chicks were also becoming much stronger. They were easily able to stride through tall grasses where only a few days before they would have stumbled or become entangled in foliage. Insects abounded in the grasses. While their parents searched for succulent herbs growing in moist pockets, the colts specialized in insect-chasing. Each was tended by one parent, who kept them well separated. This prevented the slightly older and larger colt from chasing and fighting with his younger sibling and competing with her for food. Only at night, when the female bedded down in heavy grass cover to brood them both, did the two colts come into close physical contact. One chick snuggled under each of their mother's slightly raised and folded wings. The female thus slept with her bill tucked back into her shoulder feathers. In this relaxed posture her bare crown skin was retracted into a small area above and in front of the eyes, contrasting strongly with its greatly expanded area when she was alert or frightened.

After the colts were a month old they had increased almost tenfold in weight, from five ounces to nearly three pounds, and stood nearly two feet tall. Two weeks later their flight feathers began to break out of their sheaths. By the time they were two months old they were attempting

Adult male sandhill crane and its day-old chick, lower right.

their first short flights. Almost weighing six pounds, and nearly as tall as their parents, their cinnamon downy coats had been worn away except for a few frayed wisps at the back of the head, on the back, and on the wings. The newly developing feathers looked much like those of the adults, but had tawny to rust-colored tips. Unlike their bare-crowned parents, the colts had entirely feathered crowns. When called by their parents, they quickly responded with peeping calls, but with each passing day their call seemed to acquire more of a rolling character, and began to sound like *peee-r-r-r-r*. Soon they began to take short daily flights with their parents, moving from the wooded bottomlands to the sage-covered flats near the river. There they fed while their parents spent many hours preening away their shabby and brown-stained breeding plumage to expose the incoming, smoke-gray winter plumage. Both adults had molted their flight feathers in late June, shortly after their chicks had hatched. By the time the colts fledged in late August the parents were also back in perfect flying condition.

Sandhill crane

As the warm days of August passed, the colts became increasingly strong flyers, and were progressively safer from unexpected attacks by coyotes. Thus, the birds spent ever more time foraging in the open sagebrush flats, where the youngsters ineffectively but excitedly chased grasshoppers, and the adults methodically probed the gravelly soil for fleshy bulblets and roots. Now and then a family of foraging Canada geese shared the same area, but the Canada geese were increasingly gathering into flocks and moving toward the small lakes. Each night the cranes rested in the cover of the aspens and awakened in the morning to find thin ice covering their previously invulnerable beaver-pond refuge, thus increasing the possibility of a nocturnal stalk by coyotes. Around them, the aspens were turning golden yellow and starting to drop their summer-worn leaves into the pond's dark waters.

Pair of trumpeter swans and a well-grown cygnet.

5. CHRISTIAN POND

Only a few hundred yards east of an elegant hotel overlooking Jackson Lake lies a small, shallow pond in a depression in the glacial moraine. It is annually recharged by snow melt-water, and its outlet into Christian Creek has been efficiently dammed by beavers. At its deeper southern end an extensive bed of bulrushes fringes the shoreline. The central portion is fairly deep, open water, and the northern end merges into a succession of communities dominated by emergent rushes, low grasses and sedges, and willow thickets. Thus, in a very small area a remarkably diverse and highly productive aquatic ecosystem has developed. Its architects and resident landlords are beavers who provide rent-free space from ice break-up in mid-May until freeze-up in late October. Its prime tenants are a pair of trumpeter swans.

As the pond becomes progressively ice-free in early May, the waterfowl and shorebirds that had been using Jackson Lake and the Snake River flock to the food-rich waters of Christian Pond. Mallards, pintails, American wigeons, bufflehead, Barrow's goldeneyes and ring-necked ducks are suddenly everywhere, and are quickly followed by coots and yellow-headed blackbirds. White-crowned sparrows take up territories in the peripheral sage-covered hillsides, while yellow warblers and common yellowthroats claim the willow thickets. Yellow-rumped warblers sing from the small cluster of conifers at the north end of the pond, and cliff swallows swarm over the pond by the hundred. When not feeding, they collect mud along Christian Creek to construct their nests on the under-side of the bridge that crosses the creek.

The trumpeter swans, which spent most of the winter near the oxbow of the Snake River only a mile south, moved onto the pond as soon as it started to become ice-free around the lip of the beaver dam. They immediately began investigating the dense stand of bulrushes at the southern end of the pond. Every year for more than two decades the swans had nested on the pond, usually on a mat of bulrushes from the previous year. They had raised dozens of young, which often remained in the same general area and sometimes tried to visit their parents' nesting pond. Although the pair freely mixed with their offspring on the winter-ing ponds, they would not tolerate them on their nesting territory, and greeted their recognition calls with threats or even chases. Even less toler-ated were "stranger" swans that sometimes flew overhead or attempted to land in the pond. Immediately the male would utter a challenge and take flight by running at full speed over the water toward the intruders. This was usually enough to force the birds into full flight, whereupon the male would circle back and land with a skidding stop beside its waiting mate. Facing one another in the water, they would trumpet loudly and wave their wings excitedly in a mutual triumph ceremony. By these displays the pair had managed to maintain a close bond that would last through-out their lives.

As the female, or pen, began nest construction, she trampled the bul-rushes into a well-packed mound. From this platform she reached out as far as her long neck would allow to gather additional bulrushes and add them to the mound. Soon she established a nearly bulrush-free moat around the nest as she added to its height, making it more conspicuous while providing 360° visibility. The male, or cob, assisted in a rather desultory way, generally swimming around the nest and gathering bul-rushes from beyond where the pen on the nest could reach, and dropping

Trumpeter swan adults.

them over his shoulder in the general vicinity of the nest. The pen then added them to the nest.

Within a week the nest was essentially complete, just as the pond was becoming completely ice-free. Each morning the pair spent an hour or two foraging. They also usually mated sometime during that period. Indeed, to the average observer the mating preliminaries looked no different than foraging behavior, as the swans swam side by side and repeatedly immersed their heads and necks in the water. However, their behavior gradually became more and more synchronized and increasingly began to resemble bathing movements. Soon the female lowered herself in the water and the male moved on top of her, grasping her nape in his bill and lowering his tail to meet her uplifted one. As mating terminated the pair rose strongly in the water, trumpeted loudly while spreading their wings, and then gradually settled back into normal swimming positions.

41

The pen laid her first egg on May 10 and four more on alternate days thereafter. By the 20th of May the nest cup was filled with five white eggs. As egg-laying neared completion the pen spent progressively less time away from the nest and began to add to it a sparse mixture of white down and breast feathers. Finally, after laying her last egg she settled down comfortably over the clutch and began her 34-day incubation period. At the same time the male selected a mat of bulrushes about 20 yards away as a resting and waiting station, where he could watch the nest and have an unobstructed view of the marsh and surrounding hills.

There was little danger of predation from land mammals, since disturbance of the deep water around the nest would likely deter the hungriest coyote by announcing its presence. To be sure, a watchful raven frequented the lodgepole pines at the far end of the marsh. One morning during the pen's foraging break it apparently decided to test its chances. Taking off from the trees, the raven skirted the shoreline at a height of about 30 yards, tilting its head down slightly as it passed the nest, but continuing on without veering until it reached the far end of the pond. Then, it abruptly reversed its course and, when directly above the nest again, it suddenly spiraled down toward the down-covered clutch of eggs. At that moment the cob, feeding about 50 yards away, gave a loud alarm call and began running over the water in a frantic attempt to reach the nest before any of the eggs were destroyed. Just as the raven was starting to peck at the first egg, the cob arrived at the nest. Jumping into the air, the raven eluded the swan's charge, and flew quickly to a high perch in the lodgepole pines. From there it watched as the swans performed a prolonged and noisy triumph ceremony at the nest, and the female again settled down on the undamaged clutch.

As the pen continued incubating, the marsh became a remarkably noisy place. Common snipes that had taken up territories at the meadow-like northern end of the marsh performed their daily winnowing displays. The deeper end of the pond was being fully occupied by dozens of coots and yellow-headed blackbirds. Both of these species require emergent vegetation for nesting as well as open water for foraging. The coots were

Territorial yellow-headed blackbird performing a display flight.

especially aggressive in staking out territories, often engaging in spirited battles over the choicest stands of bulrushes, with wing-beating, biting and foot-scratching. Ultimately, one combatant would get the worst of the battle and turn tail, skulking off through the reeds with its tail raised and the two white undertail patches looking like little beacons against a black background. The most aggressive males continued to cruise over their territories, with the persistence of coast-guard patrols, swimming to and fro, heads low over the water and wings lifted, challenging all comers.

The yellow-headed blackbirds likewise lost very little time initiating their breeding activities. Unlike the Brewer's blackbirds nesting in the sedge and willow flats to the north, or the redwings simultaneously taking up territories around a small, lily-covered pond to the west, tall bulrush stands are the center of the yellow-headed blackbird's world. Some 15 males were soon spread over the stand of rushes, each announcing his territorial occupancy by perching on one of the tallest rushes, spreading his tail and partially opening his wings, then bending forward, craning his neck, and uttering a hoarse, rasping call. Within a few days, females and immature males also began arriving, causing the males to rise to ever

43

greater levels of display. Each male attempted to attract more than one female into his territory if possible, but in contrast to the red-winged blackbird, many yellow-heads remained monogamous. This is probably because, unlike the red-wings, yellow-headed blackbird males regularly help gather food for the young, and particularly help feed their initial mate's brood. Thus, while red-winged blackbird males sometimes have as many as six females nesting within their territory, yellow-heads rarely have more than two.

Some late arrivals to the pond were two pairs of pied-billed grebes and a small flock of ruddy ducks. Arriving in May, the inconspicuous pied-billed grebes soon divided the pond roughly in half, one pair occupying the bulrush-filled end, and the other retreating into the shallower area, from which their calls emanated every day, but they rarely appeared in open water. By contrast, the ruddys remained in a small flock through May and well into June. The sienna-red males occasionally initiated a brief burst of display by chasing each other or jockeying for position in front of one of the nonattentive females. Once in position, the males would cock their long tails, inflate an air sac in the neck, and begin a long series of rapid tapping movements of their bills against their necks. With each stroke, the tail was more strongly cocked and air forced from beneath the breast feathers, forming a ring of bubbles around the displaying bird's breast. As the series of strokes ended, the bird pushed his cobalt-blue bill forward, opened it, and burped. The females remained magnificently indifferent to these incredible proceedings, not only rejecting the opportunity to follow the drakes, but even gaping at them if they approached too closely.

The sage-covered hills were equally alive with newly resident birds. White-crowned sparrows were especially noisy as they sang from sagebrush or low aspens only a few feet above the belt of willows lining the pond. Each white-crowned sparrow territory contained three basic elements: grass, bare ground, and shrubs. Most also included part of the shoreline of Christian Pond and often encompassed some of the taller aspens growing on the hilltop above it. The amount of grass and bare ground was always adequate to provide foraging opportunities, but not so great that the birds were unnecessarily exposed to danger. Sturdy sagebrush and other shrubs likewise provided nesting cover, but were not so dense as to separate the birds too far from their favored ground-foraging areas.

As the male white-crowned sparrows sang their plaintive whistling song repeatedly from the tops of the sagebrush, the females began wing-fluttering and uttering low, metallic trills. A male would respond by chasing the female with beak-jabbing, and by following her about persistently, singing loudly until mating occurred. A few days prior to mating the female began to pick up twigs and grasses, and even started constructing a nest in a low sagebrush bush. Within a week the nest was completed, and the first of three eggs was laid in mid-June. With completion of her clutch the female began incubating, while the male even more strongly advertised his territorial boundaries.

As June matured, the hillsides beside Christian Pond flushed golden with balsamroot, willows along its shore cast out clouds of yellow pollen, and new growth of bulrushes gradually began to hide the incubating pen swan, which had rarely left her nest for more than a few minutes since incubation had begun. She would occasionally lower her long neck to drink, but in contrast to the male, she never took long daily foraging trips to the middle of the pond where coots, ring-necked ducks, and lesser scaups foraged by the dozens. Around the margins of the pond, surface-feeding ducks such as wigeon, mallards and teal milled about. On the deepest parts, a few male Barrow's goldeneyes and buffleheads were always loafing away the days while their mates incubated clutches in hollow trees in the adjacent woods.

The pen seemed unusually restless the morning of June 24. She repeatedly stood up, lowered her bill beneath her belly, and readjusted the eggs as if to make herself more comfortable. From each egg came soft clicking sounds; the cygnets inside had broken through their air sacs and were slowly chipping away at the inner surface of the shells with their egg-teeth. As the pen rose to stretch, she dropped her wings slightly, as if to

45

Pen trumpeter swan and cygnet.

shield the hatching eggs from the sun. The cob, noticing the slight change in posture, positioned himself closer to the nest.

By evening only three of the five eggs had hatched. One had been infertile and the remaining egg had been only partially pipped before the cygnet within had exhausted its energy and died. Two of the hatched cygnets were covered with a slightly gray-toned whitish down, which graded to pure white on the front of the head and extended out on the top of the pinkish bill to a narrow point. Their large and ungainly feet were pink. The third cygnet was of the much rarer white phase, and lacked the gray tones of its broodmates. All through the evening the female sat tightly on the nest, preventing the squirming mass of cygnets below her from peeking out from beneath. Even in late June the nights of Jackson Hole are sometimes very cold, and chilling or other weather-related factors seem to be serious sources of mortality in cygnets during their first few weeks of life.

The following morning dawned clear and calm. As the morning mists slowly burned off Christian Pond, the cygnets began to peek from under the sides and rump feathers of their mother, trying to see the world about them. Early that morning the cob moved in beside the pen, and soon began to energetically clear bulrushes from around the nest. Ripping and pulling out the new growth, he piled it onto the nest, at times almost covering the cygnets. All morning he continued clearing, until by noon the nest was six inches higher, and the surrounding area was again barren of emergent plants.

The cygnets weren't the only brood to appear on the pond that day. A female Barrow's goldeneye suddenly materialized with an entourage of nine black-and-white ducklings, having brought them to the pond from their nest in a nearby hollow aspen, where they had hatched the previous day. As their mother led them out on the pond, they followed in a cluster immediately behind her, while she cleared the route of coots and ruddy ducks by threats and attacks. In her zealous efforts to attack all waterfowl in sight, she at times totally neglected her own brood, which began to scatter and lose sight of their mother. As they swam past the swan nest, plaintively peeping, both swans ignored them, and several soon became lost in the maze of bulrushes.

Near noon, the cob finally stopped his nest-building and swam away to feed, followed closely by the three cygnets. The pen remained on the nest, still covering her two unhatched eggs. Toward mid-afternoon, after carefully covering the eggs with down, she too left the nest and joined the family foraging in the middle of the pond. As the cygnets picked small invertebrates from the water surface, she and her mate reached to the bottom of the pond, pulling up pondweeds. The cygnets swam closely behind their parents, quickly consuming plant fragments and small insects brought to the surface in their parents' wake. Often one of the adults stopped to make vertical foot-paddling movements. This created strong turbulence that carried additional organisms from the bottom of the pond to the top. Small beetles, crustaceans, and insect larvae were caught by the youngsters as soon as they appeared, and the cygnets swam repeatedly from one parent to the other as they tried to satisfy their vast appetites.

As the swan brood foraged, the coots followed behind as closely as possible, picking up vegetation torn from the bottom by the swans. Wigeons and gadwalls followed slightly farther behind, always staying well out of pecking distance of the adults. By then, many of the coots were incubating full clutches in the bulrushes, and most of the male ducks were beginning to molt their colorful breeding plumage. The foraging coots were mostly pairs that had been incubating eggs since the first week in June, and the three-week incubation period was nearly over. Although the males had done most of the incubation, the females took on these duties during hatching. Since incubation began before the clutches were complete, the coot eggs hatched at different times. Within a day or two, several nests contained three or four active chicks. Then the females often called their mates to care for the remaining unhatched eggs and left with the early hatchlings. Tagging closely behind her, the grotesque golden-red and blackish chicks with scraggly down on their heads, clustered tightly about their mother as she immersed her head in the water and pulled up plants. After patiently tending the remaining eggs until most had hatched, the males too left the nest, leaving any unhatched eggs to be eaten by sharp-eyed ravens or magpies that happened to find them.

By this time, the begging sounds of young yellow-headed blackbirds in their deeply cupped and semi-domed nests produced a nearly constant background noise, interrupted by the frequent chattering of coots. Ruddy duck males, still in full breeding plumage, patrolled their bulrush-lined territories vigilantly searching for intruders, while their mates closely huddled over clutches of chalky-white eggs that seemed far too large to have been laid by them.

Every morning for the next few weeks the swan family swam from its brooding place on an old beaver lodge to the middle of the pond, with the cob in the lead, the cygnets in the middle, and the pen behind. Each day the pond's surface seemed to be increasingly occupied by new water-fowl broods and littered with feathers from molting adults. Two weeks after the cygnets had hatched, the pen began to lose her flight feathers. The male had become flightless almost three weeks earlier and was ending his molt and flightless period of about a month at the time that the female became flightless.

As July passed, the cygnets grew rapidly. From their hatching weight of seven ounces, they increased nearly tenfold their first month. By the end of August they weighed nearly sixteen pounds, a thirty-fold increase in about two-and-a-half months. By then the cygnets had attained their full juvenile plumages. Two were normal brownish-gray, but the one that had been pure white when hatched had developed into an immaculately white juvenile that was nearly indistinguishable from its parents. The calls of the cygnets also gradually changed from flute-like piping notes to more wavering calls sounding like toy trumpets, but they still lacked the volume and resonance of the adults' calls. Their bills slowly changed from pinkish to olive-black, and their legs and feet became more grayish and ultimately, black.

By early August the yellow-headed blackbirds were all fledged, the earliest of the duck broods had left the pond, and the last broods were appearing. Two female ruddy ducks emerged from their nests in dense bulrush clumps with broods of four and five young, which were miniatures of their mothers. Little heeding their mothers, the precocious ducklings soon strayed. One joined the brood of a lesser scaup, another was pecked to death when it approached too closely an adult coot feeding its young, and a third became lost and froze to death the following night. Thin ice was forming periodically along the shore of the pond, and aspens were starting to sprinkle the slopes of Lozier Hill with golden flecks. The cygnets were still a month from fledging, but were large enough to be safe from freezing or predators. Not until the end of September would they finally fledge; more than three months after hatching. Remarkably, all three survived the long fledging period; better success than most years.

6. THE OXBOW

From his perch in the tall cottonwood edging the Snake River, the male bald eagle scanned the river downstream toward the Oxbow. A half mile away a pair of ospreys was diligently fishing where the river encircles a wooded island and the main channel turns sharply southward along the base of Signal Mountain. Twelve feet below him his mate had just laid her first egg in a giant nest of twigs and branches. Both birds were nearly five years old and in full adult plumage. They had selected this nesting site the year before, spent months constructing the nest, and had gone through all the motions of breeding; but the female had not laid any eggs. After spending a month in the area, they had gradually abandoned the nest and moved to a more secluded part of the river.

It was early April, and although the river was ice-free, the land still lay under several feet of snow. The ospreys were still a month away from the start of their nesting, although last year's nest still perched conspicuously on the top of a tall lodgepole pine, only a few dozen feet from a group of equally large and also uninhabited great blue heron nests. Few of the herons had returned to the area, and none had yet attempted to establish territorial rights. Thus, the eagles and the ospreys maintained almost exclusive fishing rights to this stretch of river. To be sure, a few common mergansers sometimes patrolled its edges, and a frolicking family of otters occasionally passed downstream, but there was more than enough fish for all.

The bald eagle nest was a ponderous structure, about 60 feet up in an old and slowly dying cottonwood, which was being gradually undercut by the swift river. In March, both eagles began adding to and refurbishing their nest. They collected broken branches on the ground, or more frequently flew full force against dead branches of standing trees, breaking them off with their feet and carrying them to the nest. The largest branches, as much as three feet long and two inches in diameter, were held by the talons, while smaller ones were carried in the beak. After establishing the new nest platform, the eagles added dead grass, weeds, and clods of earth that were incidentally attached to roots. Flying over the nest with a bundle of grass in his claws, the male would drop it into the nest, while the larger female would work it into the interstices of the branches and twigs.

Within a few days they had completed a mattress-like layer of grass and straw around the raised margin of the nest surface, and by the beginning of April the nest was finally ready to receive its first eggs. Each morning during that week the female perched for a time on the tallest branches of the cottonwood. Soon the male would fly up to her, land lightly on her back, and mate with her while flapping his wings for balance. Then the female would return to her nest to further work the lining into a comfortable cup for the eggs.

She laid her first egg April 4, and two more at intervals of three days each, so that on April 10 a full clutch of three dull-white eggs were being warmed beneath her. After laying the first egg the female remained on the nest nearly constantly. Whenever she left it for any period, the male would harass and dive at her, driving her back to the nest. Soon, however, he began to help with incubation. Changeovers in nest-tending were achieved by attracting the mate to the nest with a simple chittering call.

For more than a month the two eagles guarded the nest assiduously. The first egg hatched on May 9, 35 days after being laid. The second hatched two days later, but the third embryo had died during development. As the two eaglets dried, their smoky gray body down contrasted

Adult bald eagle.

Adult bald eagle in flight.

with whitish down on the head, chin and underparts, and with a blackish bill. Weighing only three ounces at hatching, the chicks opened their eyes a few hours later and almost immediately begged for food. When the first egg hatched, the male began to bring in food, primarily suckers and other rough-fish. After dropping it into the nest both parents tore the fish into tiny bits and gently passed them to the hungry chicks. Within a week, both eaglets had grown substantially, and had even begun to wave their stubby, down-clad wings. There was plenty of food for both eaglets, but the earlier hatched bird, a female, was always fed first and soon was substantially larger than her broodmate. For the first few weeks after hatching, the female closely brooded her offspring each night, raking up the dead grass and leaves around her huddled body as the sun dropped behind Mount Moran. Her mate spent the night about twenty feet away on a higher branch of the same tree; his white head catching the last rays of the setting sun, and the feathers tinted reddish in the evening afterglow.

During the day each adult alternately foraged and tended the nest. By the end of May both eaglets were large enough to peer over the rim of the nest and watch for the arrival of their parents. As one appeared in the distance, the eaglets peeped excitedly, anticipating the feeding soon to follow. When the young were five weeks old they weighed over four pounds and were starting to replace their down with juvenile feathers. By then they could tear up their own food when it was dropped in front of them, but they could still barely rise on their toes and take a few halting steps. Most of their waking hours were spent preening and manipulating their rapidly growing primaries, which were already about half of their ultimate length. Fluffs of down from the tops of their incoming juvenile feathers lodged in the edges of the nest or were carried away by the wind until caught in vegetation or were snapped up by swallows for lining their own nests.

By their sixth week, the eaglets were fully into their brown juvenile plumages, sleek and shiny, and with their flight feathers approaching full

Bald eagle adult

length. Now the eaglets watched and waited even more impatiently as their parents constantly flew back to the nest with fish, and began screaming with excitement whenever they came into sight. Even the sight of a flying osprey carrying a fish excited them, since the adult eagles frequently dove on the ospreys until they were forced to drop their newly caught prey.

The ospreys too had been busy the past few weeks. A lightning-rent snag in a group of tall lodgepole pines on the Oxbow held a nest that the ospreys had used for several years. From it, the territorial pair could not only fish about a mile of the river and the adjoining backwaters of the Oxbow, but also could fly the short distance to Emma Matilda Lake and scan its clear water whenever the Snake River became too turbid for easy fishing.

In early April most of the great blue herons had returned either to a rookery in a streamside grove of cottonwoods immediately upstream from Moose, or to the Oxbow, where another rookery was in lodgepole pines. Over the years, heron wastes had increasingly fouled the trees and begun to kill some of them, so the remnants of the previous year's nests protruded conspicuously above the treeline. Adults of both sexes were arriving at the same time. Males that were at least three years old tried to reclaim their old nest sites, leaving the two-year-olds to try to establish territories at the edges of the colony. Gaining possession of an old nest gave a male a great advantage, since it provided the primary location from which mating displays could be performed.

One of the first males to return to the colony established his territory on the highest of the old nests and immediately began displaying. The most conspicuous of his displays was a slow, smooth lifting of his head and bill toward the vertical, stretching his neck to the utmost, and uttering a low moan. This display informed passing females of his availability for mating and would later be used as a greeting between mates during nest-building and nest-relief ceremonies. In another display, he moved his head forward while erecting the plumes of the neck, breast and body. When the neck was nearly straight, he would clack his mandibles

Ospreys at nest

Great blue heron.

together and bend his legs. This display also informed females of his availability and probably also warded off other males. Sometimes the male would take off and fly in a rather large circle while beating his wings slowly and noisily, and with his neck fully extended rather than retracted on his shoulders.

After a few days of these activities, the male finally attracted a female to his nest platform. Erecting all his plumes and standing as tall as he could, he suddenly made a bill-stabbing lunge toward the female's head, with his bill closed and his wings extended. Easily avoiding the thrust, the female simply stood her ground with open bill and awaited the next lunge. This time she simply caught the male's bill in her own and held tightly, producing a kiss-like clinch that the birds held for several seconds. After a few such exchanges the male began to tolerate his nest partner, and the female avoided most confrontations whenever the male approached too closely by keeping her eyes averted, her head low, and her crest depressed, and by industriously poking at twigs in the nest.

Soon both of them, but especially the male, were gathering sticks to bring to the nest, usually simply stealing them from nearby nests. As the male returned with a stick and passed it to his new mate, she shoved it with a trembling movement into the nest platform. No lining was added to the nest. The first egg was simply deposited on the flattened platform a few days after the female had joined and been accepted by the male. Like most other pairs in the colony, this female eventually produced three eggs, each at two-day intervals. During egg-laying the pair spent much of their time on the nest, mating frequently and often gathering additional twigs. After every mating the male flew off to get a twig to present to his mate for addition to the nest. However, after the clutch was completed and incubation began, only the incubating bird tended the nest while the other fished or stood some distance away.

The pair regularly took turns incubating. When one descended to the nest to replace its mate on the eggs, it would extend its neck, erect its crest, and call repeatedly. As it landed on the nest the sitting bird would respond with a neck-stretching display and then fly away, leaving the eggs to be tended by its mate. Often before the bird settled on the clutch, it would readjust the twigs on the platform by shoving some of their ends a bit farther into the nest or roll the eggs about with its bill.

From the start of incubation until the young were nearly three weeks old, the nest was almost never untended, for the colony was constantly watched by ravens. So long as the ospreys were close by there was little danger of raven attacks, but occasionally the entire colony would be put to flight by passing canoeists. Then the herons would race to get back to the nests first.

The osprey pair began nesting about the same time as the herons. The male arrived before the female, and immediately began to make display flights above the nesting area and add materials to the nest. Like the eagles, he sometimes broke small branches from trees while flying, but also often picked up materials from the ground. When his mate returned she too gathered nest materials, but concentrated on smaller twigs and on moss and bark for nest lining. By the first week in May they had renovated their tree-top nest.

From the time the female arrived she spent nearly all of her time tending the nest, while the male alternately gathered nest materials and fished. The birds mated frequently during this period, often on the nest, but sometimes while perched in a nearby tree. The pair initially roosted some distance from the nest at night, but the night before she laid her first egg the female remained on the nest, and deposited her first egg the next morning. Two additional eggs were laid the next several days, but from the laying of the first egg the birds never left the nest uncovered. From the first day, the male participated in incubation, but the female always spent the night on the nest and also tended it for much of the day. Thus, the male was kept busy fishing for both adults. When he returned to the nest to take over incubation he usually brought a fish for her. As he settled over the eggs, she flew to a nearby perch to consume her food.

In the third week of June, 37 days after incubation began and about 10 days after the heron eggs were hatching, the osprey eggs also hatched. They hatched in the same sequence and intervals as they had been laid, thus the oldest hatched nearly a week before the youngest. With the hatching of the first egg the male stopped nest-tending and fished full time. He brought fish to the nest and gave them to the female, who tore them into tiny pieces and carefully fed them bill-to-bill to each of the young.

As the young birds grew they were brooded progressively less by the female, but during rain or hailstorms she huddled over them and sat out the storm. During one storm the youngest and weakest chick was fatally chilled, but even with one less offspring in the nest the two remaining soon nearly filled it. After they were nearly a month old they required little parental attention. They spent much of their time viewing the heron colony activities and flapping their rapidly growing wings, attentively watched by their parents from a nearby tree.

By early August, when the eldest of the young herons were starting to take tentative flights from their nests, the osprey family was growing apace. Finally, by the middle of the month, as the young ospreys approached eight weeks old, the older one boldly climbed to an outer branch and launched itself into the air. Within a few days its younger sibling was also fledged, and thereafter the birds spent their days practicing flying skills and trying to catch fish for themselves. Often they returned to the nest to consume their prey, but as August passed, less and less time was spent in the nesting area.

Finally, by the end of August, both the osprey eyrie and the heron colony were deserted. Only the deteriorating remains of a few baby herons that had fallen from their nests and died testified that the colony had bustled with life but a few weeks earlier.

Great blue heron

Mule deer doe in aspens.

7. THE ASPEN ISLAND

Like randomly shaped pieces in a gigantic ecological jigsaw puzzle, the aspen groves of Jackson Hole form a series of golden-green islands of various sizes in a matrix of silvery green sage, and sometimes they form a narrow belt between the sagebrush flats and the darker green conifers on the mountain slopes. Each aspen grove is virtually an island unto itself, often made up of genetically identical descendants that sprout and spread from the roots of a single seedling. Sometimes a "fairy ring" of young aspens forms around an older tree or group of trees, with the ring gradually expanding at its perimeter but with the older dying aspen at the center being replaced with grass and other non-woody vegetation. More often, however, the new sprouts are avidly browsed by elk, moose and other mammals, which pull down any branches they can reach and even gnaw the bark during winter. Beavers also preferentially cut aspens for food whenever the trees are near enough to water. The older aspens are often destroyed faster than new sprouts can proliferate. Thus, many aspen islands, instead of growing and encroaching on the sagebrush flats, die out from continued browsing, and the sagebrush sea eventually covers the dead aspens.

One aspen island on a north-facing hillside overlooking the Buffalo Fork River east of Moran was the year-round home of a pair of ravens. From leaf-fall in October until the first opening of leaves and flower buds in May, the aspens stand gaunt and white against the sky, offering little cover for the ravens. Occasionally a ruffed grouse will fly up into the branches and nip off the developing buds, but the ravens depend on the vagaries of fate to provide a supply of road-killed mule deer, or they may resort to picking over the remains of elk that were killed during the hunting season or later died during the winter months.

In late February and early March the three-year-old ravens began serious work on their first nest in one of the oldest and tallest aspens at the edge of the grove, which provided unobstructed visibility of the surrounding valley. Carrying branches and sticks up to two feet long, the ravens gradually produced a bulky nest in a crotch near the center of the tree. This was lined with elk and moose hair, dried grasses, and mosses. During the warming days of March the ravens alternated between nest-building and performing courtship flights. Soaring on updrafts high above the valley, the male stayed slightly above his mate, with their wing-tips nearly touching. Then, they would dive nearly vertically for several hundred feet, the two birds tumbling over and over in the manner of tumbling pigeons, until nearly reaching the earth.

Each day the ravens ranged widely over the territory, looking over the skeletons of long-dead elk slowly being exposed by the melting snow, or picking through garbage dumps. Often they watched coyotes dig through a snowpack to expose a carcass, then they would fly to a nearby perch and wait patiently. Sometimes they had to wait until the coyote had eaten its fill, but more often they would try to sidle up to the carcass while the coyote was engrossed in its feeding. Snatching quick bites they would fly back to the nearest perch, often just out of the frustrated coyote's reach. Soon magpies would join the party, goading the coyote into endless unsuccessful efforts to keep the birds from its hard-earned meal.

Their appetites temporarily stilled, the ravens often spent time at the garbage dump in Moran, tearing up bits of paper, playing king-of-the-mountain by pushing other ravens from the tops of gravel piles, or having free-for-all chases, with the leader carrying off small articles in its bill, to be passed from bird to bird as the chase progressed.

Territorial raven atop a dead lodgepole pine.

By the middle of April their nest was nearly completed, with its cup lined with aspen bark, moose hair and grasses. By then the pair had stopped associating with the yearling and two-year-old nonbreeder flock. The male proclaimed his territory daily from the tallest trees in the aspen island, while constantly watching for intruders and noting every activity within his view. Yet, the breeding ravens were surprisingly tolerant of the nonbreeders. When a flock of these noisy and playful ravens invaded their territory, the nesting pair simply watched them in resigned silence from near their nest. But a single raven or a small group was quickly chased from the hillside. No other raven nest was within a half mile of theirs, and they quickly claimed any road-killed rodent or other food that could be readily carried away.

Within a week after adding the nest lining, the first egg was laid. Thereafter the female laid an egg each day until she had completed a clutch of six. At least one raven remained at the nest from the laying of the first egg, and the female began incubating almost immediately. Her mate

65

spent most of the day in a convenient lookout perch on a high aspen, but a few times each day the pair would fly off together to feed on a moose carcass nearby, never remaining more than about half an hour before returning to the nest.

Just three weeks after being laid, the first egg hatched, followed by four of the remaining ones on successive days. Thus, toward the end of May the nest was filled with five nearly naked young of various sizes. The remaining unhatched egg and the shells of those that had hatched were quickly removed by the female and dropped several hundred yards away, probably to reduce the chances of the nest being located by predators. Within a week of hatching, however, the nest became fouled with droppings from the youngsters and the uneaten remains of food brought to them. These included road-killed rodents, and the eggs and nestlings of many bird species, particularly of great blue herons from the Oxbow colony. This area, only four miles away from the hillside nest, was a source of food for the ravens throughout May and June. Sitting on a nearby lodgepole pine, the male raven simply waited patiently until something startled the incubating herons. Frequently it was a bald eagle flying low past their nesting colony, or a canoeist passing below. In any event, the slightest panic sent the raven into action. Flying full speed toward the nearest nest it would land on its rim about the time the heron realized what was happening and uttered its croak of alarm. Quickly piercing an egg or grabbing a nestling by the neck, the raven would drop out of sight into the trees and head back to its nest.

With such an abundance of fresh food, the young ravens grew fast, and were well-feathered by a month of age. At that age they often moved onto the edge of the nest where they would precariously perch and practice wing-flapping. The oldest sometimes ventured to the adjoining branches. One day in late June, just eight weeks after the first egg was laid, the nest was abandoned. The adults flew to a nearby tree and coaxed their unequally developed young to follow them. Although the older ones managed the flight without trouble, the youngest misjudged its

Elk calf disturbed from its hiding place in a thicket.

landing limb badly and fell with a thud to the ground. Dazed but unhurt, it managed to reach a lower branch where the rest of the family joined it.

The frightened screams of the falling young raven wakened a calf elk that had been sleeping in low brush nearby and caused its mother to look about in mild alarm. The female elk had reached this area in early June. Accompanied by her yearling offspring, she had simply separated from the herd of other pregnant females and their young of the past year, and

67

sought a sunny slope rich in greening grasses. There, early on one crisp June morning, she lay down, licked her side and genitals carefully, and within 20 minutes gave birth to her calf. Then she thoroughly cleaned it with her long tongue. Within minutes the delicately spotted calf struggled to its feet on wobbling legs and nursed. The yearling moved closer to investigate this new competitor, but the cow laid her ears back and raised one front foot and her head, an unmistakable threat that caused the confused youngster to retreat and watch from a safer distance.

After the calf nursed it dropped back down into the lush grass and slept. Its mother began grazing and moved slightly away from the resting calf. Frightened that it would be left behind, the calf tried to get up and follow, only to be pushed back down with the cow's foreleg. There it remained nearly motionless, moving only its ears to keep insects away, and letting its bright brown eyes rove as far as possible without moving its head. Every few hours the cow returned to nurse the calf, but otherwise it was left alone. There was no real danger from coyotes by this limited abandonment, since very young calves have little scent. Coyotes often would walk within a hundred yards or less of the hidden and motionless calf, unaware of its presence.

After it was about two weeks old the calf began to move about and joined a "pool" of several calves. One or two adult cows guarded the calves while the other mothers grazed. This particular pool spent most of its time at the edge of the aspen grove, where the youngsters could lie in the morning sun yet quickly retire to heavy cover if necessary.

By the time they were three weeks old the calves left the pool and moved about with their mothers. The yearlings, which learned from repeated threats or beatings to avoid associating with the mothers, formed a loose group of their own. The young males, now "spikes," sought out groups of mature males, which were also growing new antlers and were surprisingly tolerant of these newcomers.

With the increased mobility of their young, the cows became restless. Soon the entire group moved out of the aspen grove and concentrated along Buffalo Fork River before migrating toward higher summer range in the Teton Wilderness Area. There on the river bank the cows familiarized their calves with water by playing splashing games and encouraging them to run through the water. In the middle of such a game, a wandering coyote materialized close to one of the frolicking calves. Its mother quickly attacked the coyote, striking it with its front hooves. Fleeing as rapidly as possible, the coyote retreated into the safety of a mound of large rocks. Carefully sniffing the area, the cow finally discovered the hiding coyote and kicked him. The coyote then fled to a second hiding place, only to be sought out and flushed again. This time the coyote ran until it was out of sight; nevertheless the cow patrolled the area for several hours.

Finally the calves gained sufficient strength and self-confidence to allow the herd to continue its migration. Early one morning, the cows led their month-old calves to the river, followed by those persistent yearlings still showing attachment to their mothers. Encouraging the calves to enter the water, the cows crossed immediately behind and downstream from their calves, where they could readily prevent them from being swept away if they fell into deep or swift water.

As the elk crossed the river they flushed a male green-winged teal. Its mate had been incubating a clutch of eggs in a willow clump near the water until they had been found and eaten by a mink. By then, the male had already abandoned its mate. He spent his time on small gravelly islands in the river, loafing and preening free the bright feathers of his nuptial plumage, which were gradually replaced by the duller and female-like tones of his eclipse plumage. Though still functional, his flight feathers were being pushed out by the buds of the new primaries.

As the teal flew downstream, his labored flight was noted by a prairie falcon circling high above. Its eyrie, which overlooked a flat, sagebrush-covered valley, was in a rocky recess on the south-facing slope of the same hill that supported the aspen grove. The male prairie falcon had been searching for its usual food, the abundant young Uinta ground squirrels just emerging from their burrows, but the obviously troubled flight of the teal caused the falcon to veer from its course and fly parallel with the teal.

69

Female prairie falcon stooping.

Normally, the swift and agile teal was nearly on even terms with the falcon, but now it was at a distinct disadvantage, and unaware of the falcon. When it was nearly abreast of the teal, which was flying only about 50 feet above the water, the falcon partially closed its wings and dived nearly vertically, the tips of its primaries vibrating in the more than 100-mile-per-hour wind. The teal, hearing the sound, tilted his head to look upwards the instant before its back was raked by the falcon's talons with such force that the teal's neck was broken. The teal tumbled over and over to the ground beside the river, while the falcon turned quickly and followed the trail of floating feathers downward. Landing beside the dying teal, the falcon quickly killed it by biting through its neck, then covered the carcass with outstretched wings as it rested before carrying the heavy prey back to its eyrie.

The prairie falcons had nested on this hillside for many years. The shady aspen-covered northern slopes provided abundant small birds for

Prairie falcon

prey, and the sharply eroded and arid southern slopes became snow-free early in March, thus exposing a nearly vertical rock face with innumerable crevices for hiding a nest. In past years the falcons had sometimes moved their nest, usually alternating between two sites, each with sheer rock faces above, a sheltered and nearly level ledge, enough gravel for a nest scrape, and recessed enough to keep out most rain.

The two falcons wintered separately in the Green River basin, feeding mostly on horned larks, and returned to Jackson Hole in March. They immediately examined their old nest sites and renovated one of them simply by removing some debris blown in the previous autumn. Then they began a month of courtship and territorial flights, culminating in the laying of the first egg on May 4, followed by four more at daily intervals. From the laying of the first egg the female ceased to hunt. The smaller male hunted for them both. Several times a day he brought small prey to feed her, frequently mating with her during the same visit. But when the clutch neared completion and she started incubating, the male visited only occasionally, spending most of his time watching from a rocky outlook well above and about 100 yards away from the nest. Whenever he brought in fresh food for her he took over incubation while she hungrily devoured the prey.

Hunting here was superb; red-winged blackbirds were nesting along the small creek that drained the valley; the aspen grove on the other side of the hill was teeming with juncos, tree swallows and other songbirds, and Uinta ground squirrels swarmed over the valley floor. The clumsy and dull-witted ground squirrels were much easier prey than songbirds but required different hunting tactics. Instead of power diving, the falcon coursed swiftly along the ground nearly at shrub height, much like a goshawk, and knocked the rodents off their feet with a powerful blow of the talons.

About a month after incubation began, the falcon eggs hatched over a period of three days, the last on June 12. By then, many young ground squirrels were available, and the male easily provided adequate food for his larger mate and their brood.

One day the resident raven from across the hill ventured too close to the nest. The small male quickly took to the air, repeatedly uttering a hoarse alarm. Instantly the female flew from the nest in pursuit, gaining quickly on the slow-flying raven, which suddenly found itself defenseless and far from protective tree cover. As the female swooped, the raven closed both of its wings and plummeted to the ground like a rock, barely breaking its fall before hitting the rocky slope. Frantically escaping into a crevice, the raven huddled quietly as the female hawk repeatedly swooped past the opening, screaming in rage. Not until well after dark did the raven emerge and retreat quickly to its nest in the aspens, thoroughly shaken by the experience.

Prairie falcon diving

Male ruffed grouse on its drumming log in a spruce thicket.

8. THE SPRUCE FOREST

The ruffed grouse moved before dawn from his favorite roost in the aspen grove to his primary drumming log in a dense stand of tall spruce trees. Lying on the moist and still partially snow-covered soil were variably rotted logs of generations past. A carpet of soggy needles cushioned the grouse's footsteps as he approached the log in the half-light of the mid-May dawn. He lightly jumped onto the smaller end of the log and walked slowly toward its larger portion. A few feet from the end he stopped, turned his body at right angles to the log, placed his tail flush against its surface, and dug his claws tightly into the slightly decayed wood. Then, slowly at first, but with increasing speed, he thrust his open wings forward and upward, stopping them abruptly before they struck each other, and quickly returned them for the next stroke. The dull, throbbing *brum-brum-brum-br-br-brrrrrrrrrrrr* was the only sound in the hushed woods. Stopping between drumming sequences and listening intently, the male heard no challenge to his territorial proclamation. The only grouse whose territory was close to his had been killed by a goshawk only a few mornings previously. He had drummed too late in the morning to be safe. Hitting hard from behind, the goshawk knocked the grouse off his drumming log in mid-display. Only a few feathers remained scattered about the display log, which ruffed grouse had used for many years.

The spruce forest that was home and haven for the grouse and goshawk was on the Snake River floodplain near the village of Moose. The river with its cottonwood fringe comprised one boundary, while the steep slope rising to rock-strewn benches formed by earlier and higher river channels formed the other. Between them a few small creeks flowed slowly toward the river, interrupted repeatedly by beaver dams. A few of these dams created ponds sufficiently large and deep to drown the shore-line spruces and allow water lilies to grow. One such pond, Sawmill Pond, was the undisputed territory of a pair of trumpeter swans. The Colorado blue spruce forest behind it was the unassailable domain of a family of pine martens.

Marten

The marten's den was under an old deserted log cabin that in earlier days had been part of a dude ranch. The marten's home range extended from the cabin in all directions to include nearly a square mile. Within this dense spruce forest red squirrels were extremely abundant, and none was safe during the marten's daily excursions. Since the female had whelped in mid-April, she had remained in the den almost continuously, caring for the three pups. For their first month of life they nursed and slept, but did little else. At the age of five weeks they opened their eyes. The female marten, slightly smaller than her mate and with a brighter yellow chest, had depended on the male to provide food for them both. Each night the male silently left the den to search for prey. While the female was actively nursing he was forced to make several day-time excursions as well. Making a roughly circular trip through the forest, and whenever possible walking on the upper surfaces of downed trees, he would frequently pause to stand on his hind legs to survey the landscape better. The day-time trips were largely frustrating; as soon as any red squirrel saw the marten, it retreated to the highest and most secure location and uttered a piercing chattering alarm. Having thus lost its cover, the marten moved quickly along its regular train, pausing only briefly to scan the thawing surface of Sawmill Pond.

The Sawmill Pond trumpeters had nested there for many years. Lacking the dense bulrush beds of Christian Pond, Sawmill Pond nevertheless provided abundant spatterdock water lilies and pondweeds for food. As the pond became ice-free in early May, the trumpeters claimed it all for their territory. They renovated their old nest on a pile of soil and beaver-gnawed branches at the base of four flooded spruces and a living alder clustered about 20 yards from one shore. The site was ideal. The spruce trunks and alder branches nearly hid the pen while she sat on the nest, yet she needed to move only a foot or so from the nest to be in water of swimming depth where food was abundant.

Along the shore of the pond, Colorado blue spruce, lodgepole pine and narrow-leaf cottonwoods grew thick and tall. A great gray owl had a nest in one of the tallest spruces, and two pairs of ring-necked ducks had been allowed to share the pond with the swans. A mallard was nesting under a willow clump not far from the pond, and a female Barrow's goldeneye nested in a hollow cottonwood. Farther away toward the Snake River, a pair of sandhill cranes occasionally trumpeted.

Only 20 yards from the swan's nest was a large beaver lodge. It was the home of an adult male and female beaver, two two-year-old males, two young of the previous year, and a litter of three small kits born early in May. They had depleted their stored larder of willow and cottonwood branches during the long and unusually cold winter, but with the April thaw the male had been able to break through the thin ice near the lip of the dam and replenish their food supply. He also reestablished scent marks along the downstream edge of his territory where it abutted that of another colony. Every few yards along the shore he methodically spread a mixture of mud and vegetation out on the ground and deposited a few drops of oil from his castoreum gland.

After replenishing the scent marks, he began searching for food. Finding a young cottonwood about 30 yards from the dam, he stood up on his hind legs and braced himself with his tail. Then, reaching as high as possible, he cut a large bite from the side of the tree by chiseling with his two long lower incisors, with the smaller upper ones serving as a brace against which pressure could be exerted. Next, he made another cut several inches lower and wrenched out the wood between the two cuts. Then he shifted slightly to one side and repeated the process. Soon he had completely girdled the tree, and not long afterwards it fell fortuitously toward the pond. The beaver then cut away the bigger branches and hauled them to his food cache near the lodge. Hearing the tree fall, the yearling beavers soon appeared to help, and before the evening was over all that remained was the largest part of the trunk which would soon be stripped of bark and abandoned.

Also momentarily disturbed by the falling tree was a pregnant cow moose, which had been foraging with her yearling in the beaver pond. She was eight years old, and probably would not survive another year. The previous winter had ended none too soon, for she had lost much weight, and her badly worn teeth made browsing on willow shoots arduous. Her new spring pelage had finally covered all the scars left from a heavy tick infestation the previous winter and spring, but she moved ponderously through the beaver pond, as if every step was painful. The pond was the favorite part of her home range, which was only about a mile in diameter. Although many of the male moose using the same wintering area along the Snake River had moved as far as 20 miles toward higher mountain summer ranges, the female had scarcely shifted her daily pattern of activity. But she was in little danger in spite of her reduced mobility. Grizzly bears no longer regularly inhabited Grand Teton National Park, and wolves had not been seen there since the early 1900s. Barring an accident, the cow would likely survive until winter starvation or disease finally took its toll. Almost miraculously, she had become pregnant the previous November. The pregnancy had caused additional physiological stress. Now she spent most of her time standing in the shallow pond pulling up watercrowfoot and submerged pondweeds, and retiring during the hottest part of the day in the shaded spruce forest, where she could leisurely browse thimbleberry and menziesia shrubs.

The male pine marten largely ignored the beaver and the moose; neither was a threat nor a potential source of food. What the marten needed was a quick, easy kill to carry back to the den. As he climbed a spruce for a better view, his attention was drawn to a movement in a clearing near some old buildings. It was the location of a colony of Uinta ground squirrels. These common large rodents had emerged from hibernation in early April and began breeding behavior almost immediately. Two months later, in early June, the young were emerging from their holes and beginning to explore their surroundings. Gaining confidence, they ranged well away from the security of their burrows. Other than perhaps chirping in alarm, the adults largely ignored their offspring once they began their above-ground life. On this occasion a young squirrel had wandered off into tall weeds. Unable to see above the vegetation, it had no warning of the marten. In a flash the marten pounced, crushed the ground squirrel's skull instantly, and carrying its still-twitching body

79

Pine marten with the remains of a flying squirrel.

high above the ground, quickly returned to its den. The female marten greeted her mate with an excited note, and the nearly weaned litter eagerly fought over the prize that he had brought. Again the male left the den to hunt, but soon returned, this time with a junco he had chanced upon while it was incubating its nest at the base of a low shrub growing next to a lodgepole pine.

Scarcely five feet above the unfortunate junco, a female calliope hummingbird sat resolutely on her tiny nest of willow down, spider webs, bark and cone fragments, and lichens. The nest was beside two lodgepole pine cones and incredibly well hidden, looking just like another cone in the cluster. But the artistry did not end there. Besides its beautiful camouflage, a large, horizontal branch directly above the nest also hid it from above and helped to shield the incubating bird from rain. The nest tree was at the eastern edge of the forest where the earliest morning sunlight warmed the incubating female after a long and chilly night, during which her body temperature had dropped several degrees.

The female began her nest in early July when the aspens and willows were casting out great clouds of cottony seeds. The location was the same as the year before, so she merely had to renovate the old nest by raising its rim with a mixture of bark fragments and a binding of spider webs, which she wound around the nest while in flight. Next she firmly packed in a thick layer of willow down. As the nest grew to its eventual height of nearly an inch, she gathered bits of lichen from the bark of the nearby trees and neatly pasted them around its exterior with spider webbing until the whitish lining was completely obscured and the nest blended perfectly with its surroundings.

Although she mated with the same male as the previous year, this was purely by chance, since hummingbirds don't establish the monogamous pair bonds common to many other birds. The female, in seeking out her old nesting tree, had simply entered the territory of the same male that had defended the forest edge the previous year.

Indeed, the male even perched in his usual position on top of a moose-browsed willow where the tiny creature had a commanding view of the

81

"As the young calliope hummingbirds reached the end of their third week of life, they could hardly be distinguished from their mother."

clearing. Periodically he drove away any intruding male hummingbirds, including the larger black-chinned species, which sometimes flew into the meadow to feed on the abundant Indian paintbrush flowers just blossoming. Frequently, too, he sallied out to capture a passing insect. Sometimes even a robin would be persecuted by the diminutive bird, with the male towering high in the air before diving down on the confused intruder, which simply chose to disappear into the heavy forest rather than try to defend itself.

Whenever not occupied with such activities, the male watched closely for any female hummingbirds attracted to the Indian paintbrushes and scarlet gilias. With the first arrival of a female, the male instantly flew off, gained altitude, and hovered almost 75 feet above her, orienting himself so the sun reflected from his iridescent throat gorget toward the foraging female. Suddenly the tiny and inconspicuous object in the sky was transformed into a beam of ruby light. Then, shooting downward at full speed in a broad arc, he passed only a few feet above the female. Pulling out of his dive and soaring up again, he completed the arc, again hovering and flashing his gorget toward the female. After three such performances, the male landed on a nearby perch and continued to expose his magnificent coloration to her view. This female had not yet begun to nest and was receptive to his attentions. Thus, within a few days, two females were nesting within his territory, yet he continued to look for more.

The female incubating the first nest tended its two eggs almost without interruption for fifteen days. Taking short breaks to feed only during the warmest part of each day, she was showing signs of exhaustion. Only the night before she sat tight on the nest throughout a violent wind, hail, and rainstorm, with her needle-like bill pointed directly upwards and her wings spread over the nest cup to form a tiny cone off which the raindrops flowed. Amazingly, she and her eggs had survived the storm. Indeed, the eggs soon hatched. After they had finally kicked themselves free of their shells, the babies lay motionless on the floor of the nest, no larger than peas, virtually naked, and totally blind. Their tiny yellow bills were short instead of needle-like, yet they could gape, and when they did the female carefully inserted her long tongue into their throats and regurgitated a mixture of nectar and tiny insects.

As the days passed, the babies slowly assumed a more recognizable form, and within ten days they were finding the tiny nest cup too small. By then, they were impossible to brood, even at night. As they grew, the combined bulk and weight of female and her young started to flatten the nest. By the time the babies were two weeks old they could remain on it only by standing side by side. The female was constantly busy bringing them nectar and insects, sometimes temporarily storing the insects in her throat, but often carrying them in her bill and passing them directly to the youngsters.

As the young hummingbirds reached the end of their third week of life, they could hardly be distinguished from their mother. Now they spent much of their time flexing and tentatively vibrating their wings, and carefully venturing out on the branch beside their fully flattened nest. As one of the young thus exercised, it "raced" its wings more strongly than usual, and briefly rose a few inches above its perch. Momentarily frightened, it settled back on the branch. But a few minutes later it tried again, and this time, rather than simply rising vertically like a helicopter, it shifted into forward gear and sped to a nearby branch. There it landed and rested, while the other youngster watched. Later that day it too took off for the first time, and by the following day the nest was abandoned.

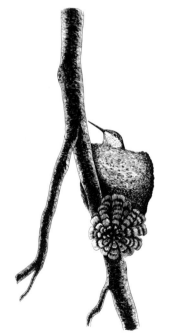

Calliope hummingbird female and nest

9. THE CIRQUE

The little lake remained tightly ice-bound in the spring sunshine, even though patches of green were appearing around its edges, and white calthas and yellow avalanche lilies were poking their perennially optimistic blossoms through the quickly melting snow. Around the snow-hidden circular lake, named Solitude by some unknown explorer, a spectacular amphitheater rises sharply for nearly 1,000 feet. It closely clasps the lake in its rocky grasp except to the southeast where the walls open to provide a stunning vista of a triumvirate of massive pinnacles, the Grand Teton, Mount Owen, and Teewinot Mountain. Melting snow and ice from the slopes of the rocky cirque feeds the lake and, in turn, a tiny creek that flows steeply down Cascade Canyon to spill into Jenny Lake five miles away and more than two thousand feet lower. Along the way, the stream tumbles through a magnificent forest-edged canyon, gaining strength from innumerable rivulets leaping down the mountainsides. A massive glacier once bulldozed down the same canyon, crudely gouging it into a broad, U-shaped valley. Now, however, the stream is only a few feet across in many places, and choked with boulders and fallen trees. Small waterfalls commonly toss the stream into spray and foam.

One of these is a free-fall of about 10 feet where a rocky outcrop slowed the cutting edge of the creek. A small gray bird occasionally burst out from behind the streaming water like a shot from a hidden cannon, or just as surprisingly flew full-force into the misty spray from downstream.

The pair of dippers that had built their nest behind the falls ranged up and down a half-mile of Cascade Creek, strenuously defending their territory from other pairs upstream and downstream from them. They were intimately familiar with every twist and turn of their part of the creek, but virtually everything beyond it was *terra incognita*. The dippers invariably followed the winding stream when flying up or down it and rarely flew more than a few feet above the swirling waters.

During winter the dippers moved downstream toward Jenny Lake, but in spring they returned to their previous territory. Even before returning, the male began singing exuberantly. Indeed, both members of the pair sang loudly from January on, usually while perched on a rock in the middle of a stream, but the male was especially vocal while in the presence of his mate. At times they engaged in spirited chases, the male singing loudly while flying closely behind the female, who twisted and turned as if trying to escape, but who goaded the male to chase her whenever he seemed to tire of the game. Sometimes they collided in mid-air and tumbled together into the water, but mating occurred on a sandbar after the pair alighted there normally.

Their nest had been in the same location for several years. The dippers simply repaired it each year by adding grass and moss. It was a simple globular structure about the size of a football, with a downward-pointing entrance hole that opened toward the falling water. In fact, the outside of the nest was constantly moistened by the spray. But within this soggy structure was a cup of coarse, water-resistant grasses, and a dry inner lining of leaves. Within a few days of replacing the inner lining, which the pair had removed the previous summer as soon as the young had fledged, egg-laying began. One egg was laid on each of four successive days.

Throughout this time, both dippers spent most of their time foraging in the rushing stream, by flying headlong into the icy waters. As they entered the water they threw their wings out and back slightly and swam quickly to the stream bottom. They worked their way upstream by walking and using their wings, picking among the rocks for stonefly and mayfly larvae, and occasionally also taking small fishes. When they had trouble finding food they sometimes remained submerged for 15 or 20 seconds, but often popped back up to the surface after only 5 or 10 seconds.

After completing her clutch, the female abandoned her food searches and incubated full-time. The male was forced to work ever harder to obtain enough food for himself and his mate, since he fed her on the nest while she incubated. With the hatching of the young after some 16 days of incubation, the situation changed. The female gradually assumed the initiative in food-getting, although she also brooded a good deal of the time the first week after hatching. With room for only one adult on the nest, the female would rise on her legs far enough to let the young poke their heads out from beneath her to receive their food when the male appeared at the nest opening. Frequently he carried a fecal sac away from the nest, but within a week after hatching the young birds began to extrude their capsules directly out the nest opening into the water below.

By then the young were extremely vocal, calling for food so loudly that they could be heard over the roar of the waterfall. Their dark, beady eyes watched every movement through the peephole in their nest. They had been in the nest for three weeks, and had become so crowded that they could hardly move by the time they were 24 days old and finally ready to leave the nest. As their parents watched and called from below, the young birds fluttered down from the nest one by one. Although their wings were well grown, their tails were still fairly stubby. They moved awkwardly about the edge of the pool at the waterfall's base, testing the water with their toes, poking their heads underwater, and bathing in the shallows. But most of the time they explored the rocks around them, falling into crevices, climbing steep banks, and generally testing their coordination.

Beside the cirque-enclosed lake, where the sound of the distant waterfall was barely audible, the silence was occasionally broken by the groaning of heaving ice and by a plaintive bleating from near a boulder at the foot of a talus slope, where the rubble of uncounted millenia of erosion had come to rest in an uncertain truce with gravity. The face of the boulder jutted out toward the top, forming a parapet below which was somewhat sheltered from the wind and rain. Peering out occasionally from this refuge was a rodent-like animal with stubby ears, an almost non-existent tail, and short legs that looked as if they had been designed for an animal half its size. It was a pika, a distant relative of rabbits, that lived under the boulder. Its den was at the bottom of the rock slide. An indistinct pathway led from the boulder field to a meadow about 40 feet away. Scattered near the den were the remains of several piles of hay that had been gathered the previous summer and fall for consumption over the long winter.

Most of the haystacks were relatively exposed rather than hidden under boulders, and were comprised of grasses, herbs and even a few sprigs of Douglas fir and aspen. Scattered on the tops of some stacks were the dried scats of yellow-bellied marmots, which the pika had apparently also gathered to consume with the nutritious grasses and herbs.

The owner of this particular haystack eyed his diminishing pile of food and made a tentative survey trip toward the meadow. The soggy ground was still mostly snow-covered. It would be at least another month until the new growth of grasses and sedges would be high enough to warrant gathering. Until then the male had to simply defend his territory of about a tenth of an acre from other pikas, primarily by advertising his claim with repeated "ank" calls.

Below the rocky outlook and several feet back from its opening lay a female pika with a litter of three. They had been born early in the spring, and by early June were virtually weaned and showing signs of independence. Within a month they would be expelled from their comfortable burrow, and forced into trying to establish their own territories and gather enough hay to carry them through the long winter. But for now, at least, they basked in the comfort and warmth of their mother's body, scarcely aware of the persistent territorial calling of their father.

The male, between calling bursts, sunned himself from the top of his favorite boulder, which had become extensively white-stained with dried urine and littered with tiny round droppings at its base. Suddenly rocks

Pika

clattered above, and the startled pika jumped back into the safety of his rocky refugium. Peering carefully out, he saw a ram bighorn sheep clambering up the rocky slope 500 feet above, kicking small rocks loose to tumble noisily downward until coming to rest on the talus slope.

The ram was part of a small group that had wandered east over the crest of the Teton Range from their usual home on its western slopes. They had spent the late winter on the steepest south-facing slopes of the cirque, where snow couldn't accumulate to great depths and where the weak winter sun tended to melt it sooner than on the more sheltered northern or western slopes of the cirque. As spring slowly came to the alpine zone, the retreating snow line erratically moved up the slope and around to these protected exposures, but the first greenery was to be found on the steep southern ledges. The females had wintered separately from the rams and left the wintering areas about a month earlier to return to their traditional lambing areas several miles away. Most had become pregnant during the fall rut, and by late winter they began to ignore their own lambs of the previous year. A few of these allowed themselves to be "adopted" by lambless females. Others associated with the rams, but all were tolerated by all of the older sheep.

Several older rams bore splintered horns and scars from the terrible fighting of the past rutting season, which began in November and peaked in December. Then the mountains fairly rang with the crashing head charges of rams fighting to establish dominance. Much of the fighting occurred shortly after the rams moved to their rutting grounds, but occasionally even in late spring dominance fights developed whenever two strange rams happened to meet. Facing each other on the steep slope, two rams would approach with head low and neck stretched forward, until they were close enough to kick forward and upward with one of their forelegs, striking each other on the chest or belly. Then, slowly moving past each other with their heads held low and noses almost touching the ground, they would pace off several steps, suddenly whirl, rise on their hind legs, and bring all of their weight and strength downward and forward in a skull-jolting clash. Time and again they would strike each other, until one accepted defeat by behaving submissively like a female, quietly accepting the kicks, threats, and sometimes even the sexual advances of the other ram. These dominance battles were not engaged in to acquire a harem, but to allow uncontested access to females during their very limited period of sexual receptivity.

As the pregnant ewes left their wintering areas for their lambing grounds, they remained together until about two weeks prior to giving birth. Then they separated to seek sheltered sites in extremely steep and rough terrain. This reduced the probability of predation on the ewes and their newborn lambs during this vulnerable period. But the lambs were very alert and active almost from the moment of birth. As the ewes licked their lambs dry, they learned their special scent that thereafter enabled each ewe to recognize her lamb. From that time on no other lamb would be accepted for nursing. Likewise, within a few days after birth each lamb learned to recognize its own mother, but by visual rather than scent characteristics.

About a week after giving birth, the ewes led their lambs back to the group of lambless ewes and juvenile sheep. The lambs soon formed nursery groups and spent much of their time playing, fighting, and frolicking about the mountain slopes.

During the first month or so of their lives, the lambs remained together in their nursery herd, roaming about with the ewes. All returned periodically to their mothers to nurse, but were otherwise left largely to themselves without special attention from their mothers or other ewes. By late summer the lambs' baby coats began to be replaced by darker, adult-like pelage, and they were also gradually being weaned. From then on the ewes showed little interest in their own offspring. Nevertheless, when the herd moved toward their late summer foraging areas, each lamb followed dutifully behind its mother and would continue to do so until the following spring.

As the lambs charged and clashed with one another on a rock-strewn alpine meadow, they scarcely heard the excited calls of a male black rosy finch whose mate had a nest in a crevice of a nearly vertical rock face.

The pair had reached the area in May when the cirque was still mostly ice and snow-covered. They soon began courtship activities in spite of their bleak surroundings. Holding his tail almost perpendicularly over his back, the male extended and vibrated his wings while lowering his head and pointing his bill skyward. As the male chirped almost continuously in this extreme posture and held a bit of grass in his bill, the female adopted a very similar posture and was almost immediately mounted by the male.

Soon the pair sought out a nesting territory. They concentrated their searches on a deep, 30-foot crevice in the mountain that provided protection from wind, snow and rain. Selecting a site about halfway up the crevice, the female carried grasses to a tiny ledge about five inches back from the opening. Within a few days she fashioned a deeply cupped nest of grass on a mossy base, and added a soft lining of mountain sheep hair. On the first day of summer the nest had a full complement of five white eggs, all laid within a week.

During most of this time the male had been kept busy defending the female from the attentions of unmated males, for there was a considerable excess of males. However, once incubation started he had little to do except when the female interrupted her nest-tending to forage. Then he would once again drive other males away from their foraging grounds. Early in the summer the birds had eaten seeds remaining from the past year, but as June gradually passed more and more insects appeared. Many were carried upwards by the wind and deposited numb and helpless on the snow. When the young hatched in early July, there was an abundance of insect food to be gathered for them. Initially the female did all the feeding as well as all the brooding of the young. However, about a week after hatching the male also began feeding the demanding babies. They did not try to venture from their nest until they were nearly three weeks old. By then they had acquired a gray and buffy plumage. It matched the surrounding rocks so well that the young could hardly be seen when they were immobile. By late August all the animals in the cirque were basking in the life-giving sunshine of the all-too-brief alpine summer.

10. THE END OF SUMMER

 August is the time of warm days and easy living for animals in Jackson Hole. Mosquitoes that had plagued the birds and large mammals during June and early July disappear, and an abundance of food makes foraging almost a spare-time activity rather than the central preoccupation of life.

The young pine martens were almost grown and soon began to hunt with their parents. Usually the family was up by dawn, with the young eager to be out. The youngsters delighted in racing up and down an old cottonwood near their den, playing games of tag. At times they jumped from the lower branches to the ground, or they would hang on to them with only their forelegs or hindlegs. Or, they would roll about on the ground in mock-fighting, snarling and growling ferociously, but never really hurting each other. When they had nothing more exciting to do they stalked grasshoppers and ate them with apparent delight. But by and large they still depended on food caught for them by the adults, which ranged from ground squirrels, flying squirrels, and chipmunks to occasional animals as large as marmots and snowshoe hares. During the middle of the day, when their prey was mostly under cover, the family sometimes returned to the coolness of their den or any other shade. Then the young martens would take a short nap curled up beside each other, with their tails wrapped around their noses.

Male pine marten.

By the middle of August the female marten was again coming into heat. She soon began to utter clucks that tended to attract the male, and to make scent markings by urinating or rubbing her belly on various objects near their den. She also became much more aggressive toward her mate, at times treating his approaches with tail-twitching and wrestling, although she was only about two-thirds as large as he. But the male was equally rough with her, often dragging her about before mating with her, with the skin of her neck in his mouth. Afterward, they would peacefully associate, as if unmindful of their struggling and fighting only a few minutes previously.

Nearby, the beaver lodge was also the scene of summer ease. During most of the day the beavers were sound asleep or resting. Toward the end of the day they would awaken, leave the lodge, and spend the night repairing the dam, feeding, and loafing, returning to their lodge about sunrise. The baby beavers were more reluctant than the adults to retire

94

for the day, and they often whined in protest before falling off to sleep. They were also the last to wake up and begin their evening activities.

As each beaver awoke it would stand up, often bumping its head on the roof of the tiny lodge chamber, and step out almost noiselessly through the exit hole into the water. Swimming out about 20 feet it would turn around, return to the nest chamber, and shake itself free of water. After each animal thus freshened itself it would again leave the lodge and begin foraging for an hour or more. It was still too soon for the beavers to begin storing food for the winter, and so these foraging trips had no sense of urgency. Frequently, in fact, the beavers would simply sit for a time on the top of the lodge before going out to feed, or perhaps swim for awhile in aimless circles as if enjoying the exercise. All the beavers knew the location of every aspen tree within several hundred yards of the pond, and they would often bypass stands of willows and alders to enjoy this delicacy. A beaver might spend an hour or more feeding on an aspen tree before going elsewhere. If one beaver started cutting down a tree, the others never helped until the tree had been felled. Then the other lodge members would quickly appear to help cut it up. Soon the larger branches would be dragged to the water. Their bark and leaves would provide food for several days. Next, the smaller part of the trunk would be cut into pieces and pulled to the water, but the largest parts of the trunk would eventually be abandoned.

When the kits were still young they typically stayed in the lodge all night while their mother towed in leaf-laden branches for them to eat inside. As they grew older, their mother delayed more and more this delivery of their food. Soon they began to venture out on their own, and by mid-August the mother rarely brought food to them. The first kit initially ventured out with its mother when it was almost two months old. As it cautiously swam toward the shoreline, its mother followed closely behind with her chin resting on the end of the kit's tail. At times the kit hesitated, and would turn back to its mother to touch its chin against her head. Then, gaining confidence, it tentatively dived. As soon as it emerged, the mother caught up with it, and they once again continued their exploration of the pond.

95

The youngster soon tired and repeatedly turned back toward its mother and tried to climb on her back. After enduring this for a few minutes, the mother simply dived and left the kit to swim on its own. As the two animals reached the shoreline the mother left the water to gather leafy vegetation for her kit. It remained in the shallow water, whining with discontent until she appeared with a leafy aspen branch. Then it avidly grabbed the branch with its forepaws and stuffed the succulent leaves in its mouth, almost ignoring the larger twigs and branches.

Little attention was paid the kits by their father and the immature beavers. They seemed to go their various ways when foraging and repairing the dam or lodge. None ever overtly helped another in these tasks, but each seemed to recognize that these duties had to be done if their limited world was to remain intact.

As summer passed, the two two-year-old males became increasingly restless and were tolerated progressively less by the adult male. He frequently chased them from favored food supplies or threatened them when one approached too close to him. Before the summer was over, the two immature males would be evicted from the lodge. Then they might have to travel several miles upstream or downstream in search of undefended areas of shoreline where they could try to establish a den prior to the coming winter. This would be a very difficult time for them compared with their previous life of relative leisure. The youngsters would be exposing themselves to unknown dangers such as otters and minks in the new habitats, and also would have to gather enough food for the long winter ahead. They would then have to try and locate mates to help them in the arduous task of dam and lodge construction.

With the end of August, the aspens were slowly becoming transformed into golden torches, and the forest edges and the lakeshores were aflame with the scarlet leaves and berries of the mountain ash. The beavers would soon lose their worn summer coats and replace them with the longer and more luxuriant winter pelage. Likewise, the pine martens were gradually replacing their now rough and grizzled summer fur with their stunning winter coats of longer and more lustrous reddish brown upper coloration, a more blackish tail and legs, and an orange-yellow throat patch.

By early September the change of seasons was evident almost everywhere. Already the snowline was progressing perceptibly down the slopes of the Grand Teton, and the golden belt of aspens around the rim of Jackson Hole filled the entire area with a radiance almost beyond credulity. The trumpeter swans cygnets on Christian Pond were nearly fledged and spent long periods flapping their wings in exercise. The sand-hill crane family from the beaver pond in the willow thicket had fledged in late August. Together with cranes from elsewhere in the Park, they gathered in open meadows prior to leaving for their Bear Lake fall staging areas. The heron colony on the Oxbow was likewise deserted, the last of the young having fledged in mid-August, about the same time that the ospreys on the Oxbow abandoned their eyrie.

In high mountain meadows, the elk were also responding to the first signs of autumn. Gradually, as the nights became colder and vegetation on parts of the summer range dried out, the herds began to break up and move to lusher vegetation and lower areas. Since early August the males had been rubbing velvet from their hardened antlers by thrashing shrubs and weeds, which also tended to release some of the aggressive energy building within them.

The first indication that the rut was approaching was the growing intolerance of the older bulls toward younger ones, which after a few threats moved off to the edge of the bull groups. A few spikes that had remained with their mothers began driving the older cows about, even attempting to bugle, but the cows largely ignored them. Here and there older bulls began to bugle, but the cows also avoided their efforts to gather them together and hold them in a group.

As the days continued to grow colder and the elk moved to progressively lower meadows, the older bulls' tempers also grew shorter. Each spent more time driving the cows, thrashing the vegetation, and wallowing in muddy or boggy areas. Although the bulls bugled throughout the day, they concentrated their bugling in the morning and evening, chal-

97

Cow elk in a mountain meadow.

lenging all others within hearing. Soon, the largest and most dominant males controlled a dozen or more cows and their calves, constantly driving and patrolling them and grazing but little.

For the elk, this was the start of an intensely dangerous period. To reach the safety of their winter range, they would have to run the gauntlet of nearly 1,000 hunters within Grand Teton National Park, and

98

other hundreds in the adjoining Bridger-Teton National Forest. The bull hunting season in the National Forest usually begins in early September during the rut. To survive the early fall hunt, bulls must remain in the most remote high country for as long as possible. Yet, when winter finally forces them out of the high wilderness areas before the hunting season ends, most bull elk must face a firing line of hunters along roads in the park. The trip can be made safely only at night or by remaining as long as possible west of the Snake River where hunting is not allowed. Yet, for the ultimate good of the elk and the entire ecosystem, their numbers must not be allowed to outstrip the resources of the wintering grounds. The bloody scenes reenacted every fall in parts of Grand Teton National Park are the unhappy solution adopted, for better or worse, by the state and federal agencies responsible for management of the elk and their habitat.

In such questions lies the paradox of preserving and protecting the wildlife, and the complex inter-relationships that hold the ecosystem together. To preserve the elk from all hunting is to invite disaster by their over-browsing of plants such as aspen upon which so many other animals depend so heavily. Humans have already eliminated wolves and nearly eliminated mountain lions that once helped control the elk population. The winter range will only support a limited population, leaving the rest to die, whether from periodic disease, starvation, or hunting.

The life of Grand Teton National Park is thus a continuing challenge to the intellect. Since we cannot "control" the elk without inadvertently affecting the ravens, coyotes and aspens, so we cannot affect coyotes or aspens without also affecting mice and tree swallows. And we cannot affect tree swallows in the Tetons without affecting them in their wintering areas in Central America. In this way, the world is drawn ever closer together, and the shockwaves of how we act here and now will emanate in time and space, as the ripples of the present spread out to touch and disturb the shorelines of the future. Thus the cranes that nest on an old abandoned beaver lodge are as dependent upon the now-dead beaver as the moose or swan that forages in the beaver pond, or the osprey that fishes in its clear waters. And the swan killed by a frustrated elk hunter who failed somehow to get "his" bull is not only gone for all time, but its lifelong mate and their potential future broods are also effectively eliminated. And so their pond lacks the trumpeting calls that carry with them all the majesty of 50 million years of swan evolution and survival, leaving only the silent mountains to endure.

For whatever values and purposes we might seek in wild animals we must ever try to comprehend them better; they will never comprehend us. We must also love them for what they are, whether large or small, beautiful or ugly, predator or prey, for they will never love us. And we must try to preserve them from extinction for our own good, for we control the destinies of all species in the animal kingdom.

Bull elk

Wildlife Observations in Grand Teton National Park

The great diversity of wildlife in the Park insures interesting observations any time of the year. However, some areas and seasons are better than others. Throughout the year, early morning and late evening are the best times to see large animals. Late spring (mid-May to early June) and late fall (September and October) are also generally better than mid-summer, when heavy traffic and human disturbance tend to keep large animals away from well-travelled areas.

Elk may be seen most of the year at the National Elk Refuge near Jackson, with several thousand there from late November or December through April. During summer, elk usually can be seen in the Park toward sunset from the dirt road south of Signal Mountain and near Timbered Island.

Moose are usually readily found throughout the year in marshes and extensive willow stands. The willow flats east of Jackson Lake and the bottomlands of the Snake, Gros Ventre and Buffalo Fork Rivers are favored by moose.

Pronghorn are most often seen on Antelope Flats and east of Blacktail Butte during summer, and usually are visible from U.S. highway 26-287 or the Antelope Flats Road. They are sometimes also observed along the Gros Ventre River east of the Park.

Bison in the Park number between 30 and 40, and rarely stay in any area very long. During summer and fall they mostly range the sagebrush flats west of the Snake River between Jackson Lake and Moose, especially the Potholes area. They are sometimes also seen in the lower Gros Ventre valley, particularly during early summer.

Mountain Sheep are not abundant and are most readily seen during winter in the Red Hills area along the Gros Ventre River east of the Park and in the

National Elk Refuge. They also make rare appearances on Sheep Mountain year-round and in the Teton Range during summer.

Coyotes may be seen almost anywhere, but most often in open meadows during early morning and late evening. They are especially common on Antelope Flats. During winter they concentrate on the National Elk Refuge.

Mule Deer are widely distributed in the Park, and are infrequently seen along the trails in the Teton Range. They are also relatively common along the shore of Jackson Lake, and on the slopes of Signal Mountain and Blacktail Butte.

Black Bears are not numerous in the Park, but sometimes are seen near many of the campgrounds. They are also occasionally seen in the foothills and canyons of the Teton Range.

Bald Eagles can usually be found along the Snake River, and are often seen on float trips down the river. Usually at least one pair nests in the Park. Disturbing their nests is prohibited, and river floaters are not allowed to land near nesting areas.

Ospreys are also frequently seen along the Snake River, with several pairs nesting from the Oxbow south. They also nest along the shores of Jackson, Leigh and Jenny Lakes.

Trumpeter Swans are frequently seen on Jackson Lake and the Snake River during the non-breeding season, and during summer are found on Christian Pond, Sawmill Pond, and several of the more inaccessible beaver ponds or lakes throughout the valley areas of Jackson Hole. Usually at least one nesting pair, and sometimes small flocks of nonbreeders, can be seen at the National Elk Refuge.

Greater Sandhill Cranes are most often seen on the National Elk Refuge from the highway near Jackson. They also frequent the Oxbow area of the Snake River and the willow flats east of Jackson Lake. During the nesting season sandhill cranes are intolerant of humans, and must not be disturbed.

Great Blue Herons may be easily seen during the nesting season from the highway at the Snake River Oxbow. A second heronry is along the Snake River north of Moose and near the Blacktail Pond overlook.

Other animals, such as weasels, pine martens, snowshoe hares and porcupines are scattered throughout the coniferous forests at unpredictable locations. River otters are most often seen in the Snake River, and beavers can usually be seen during evening along the River or on ponds at numerous places in the Park. Pikas and yellow-bellied marmots are commonly seen on talus slopes in canyons of the Teton Range.

Golden eagle

A Checklist of Vertebrates of Grand Teton National Park

Birds*

Common Loon (*Gavia immer*). Occasional in spring and fall, rare in summer.

Red-necked Grebe (*Podiceps griseigena*). Accidental in spring.

Horned Grebe (*Podiceps auritus*). Accidental in fall.

Eared Grebe (*Podiceps nigricollis*). Occasional to rare from spring to fall.

Western Grebe (*Aechmophorus occidentalis*). Rare from spring to fall.

Pied-billed Grebe (*Podilymbus podiceps*). Uncommon to rare from spring to fall, breeding in the Park.

White Pelican (*Pelecanus erythrorhynchus*). Variably common from spring to fall, but not breeding in the Park.

Double-crested Cormorant (*Phalacrocorax auritus*). Occasional in spring and fall.

Great Blue Heron (*Ardea herodius*). Present throughout year but rare in winter, breeding locally in the Park.

Common (Great) Egret (*Egretta alba*). Accidental in spring.

Snowy Egret (*Egretta thula*). Rare from spring to fall, not known to breed in the Park.

Black-crowned Night Heron (*Nycticorax nycticorax*). Accidental in spring and fall.

American Bittern (*Botaurus lentiginosus*). Uncommon from spring to fall, breeding in the Park.

White-faced Ibis (*Plegadis chihi*). Occasional in spring.

Whistling Swan (*Cygnus columbianus*). Accidental or occasional during spring, fall and winter.

Trumpeter Swan (*Cygnus buccinator*). Common throughout the year, breeding in the Park.

---

*Based primarily on *Birds of Jackson Hole* by B. and G. Raynes, 1979, with minor modifications.

Canada Goose (*Branta canadensis*). Common throughout the year, breeding in the Park.

White-fronted Goose (*Anser albifrons*). Accidental in fall.

Snow Goose (*Anser caerulescens*). Occasional in fall, rare during winter.

Mallard (*Anas platyrhynchos*). Common to abundant throughout the year, breeding in the Park.

Gadwall (*Anas strepera*). Uncommon summer breeder, common spring and fall migrant, rare in winter.

Pintail (*Anas acuta*). Uncommon summer breeder, common spring and fall migrant, uncommon in winter.

Green-winged Teal (*Anas crecca*). Common to uncommon throughout the year, breeding in the Park.

Cinnamon Teal (*Anas cyanoptera*). Uncommon breeder and migrant in spring and fall.

American Wigeon (*Anas americana*). Uncommon summer breeder, common in spring and fall, and rare in winter.

Shoveler (*Anas clypeata*). Rare to occasional throughout the year, probably breeding in the Park.

Redhead (*Aythya americana*). Uncommon summer breeder, common to rare migrant in spring and fall.

Ring-necked Duck (*Aythya collaris*). Common to uncommon throughout the year, breeding in the Park.

Canvasback (*Aythya valisineria*). Occasional spring and fall migrant.

Lesser Scaup (*Aythya affinis*). Occasional spring and fall migrant.

Common Goldeneye (*Bucephala americana*). Occasional throughout the year.

Barrow's Goldeneye (*Bucephala islandica*). Common to uncommon throughout the year, breeding in the Park.

Bufflehead (*Bucephala albeola*). Rare to occasional throughout the year, breeding rarely in the Park.

Harlequin Duck (*Histrionicus histrionicus*). Occasional from spring to fall.

White-winged Scoter (*Melanitta deglandi*). Accidental in fall.

Surf Scoter (*Melanitta perspicillata*). Accidental in fall.

Ruddy Duck (*Oxyura jamaicensis*). Occasional from late spring to fall, breeding in the Park.

Hooded Merganser (*Lophodytes cucullatus*). Rare from fall to spring.

Common Merganser (*Mergus merganser*). Common throughout the year, breeding in the Park.

Red-breasted Merganser (*Mergus serrator*). Occasional in spring and fall.

Turkey Vulture (*Cathartes aura*). Rare from spring to fall.

Goshawk (*Accipiter gentilis*). Common to uncommon throughout the year, breeding in the Park.

Sharp-shinned Hawk (*Accipiter striatus*). Occasional from spring to fall.

Cooper's Hawk (*Accipiter cooperi*). Occasional from spring to fall.

Red-tailed Hawk (*Buteo jamaicensis*). Common from spring to fall, breeding in the Park, rare in winter.

Swainson's Hawk (*Buteo swainsoni*). Common from spring to fall, breeding in the Park.

Rough-legged Hawk (*Buteo lagopus*). Common from fall to spring.

Ferruginous Hawk (*Buteo regalis*). Rare throughout the year.

Golden Eagle (*Aquila chrysaetos*). Occasional throughout the year.

Bald Eagle (*Haliaeetus leucocephala*). Common throughout the year, breeding in the Park.

Marsh Hawk (*Circus cyaneus*). Occasional from spring through fall, rare in winter.

Osprey (*Pandion haliaetus*). Common from spring through fall, breeding in the Park; rare in winter.

Prairie Falcon (*Falco mexicanus*). Occasional from spring through fall, breeding in the Park.

Peregrine Falcon (*Falco peregrinus*). Rare throughout the year.

Merlin (*Falco columbarius*). Occasional in spring and fall.

American Kestrel (*Falco sparverius*). Common from spring to fall, breeding in the Park; rare in winter.

Blue Grouse (*Dendragapus obscurus*). Common throughout the year, breeding in the Park.

Ruffed Grouse (*Bonasa umbellus*). Common throughout the year, breeding in the Park.

Sage Grouse (*Centrocercus urophasianus*). Common throughout the year, breeding in the Park.

Chukar (*Alectoris chukar*). Accidental in fall and winter.

Sandhill Crane (*Grus canadensis*). Uncommon from spring to fall, breeding in the Park.

Whooping Crane (*Grus americana*). Accidental in spring and fall.

Virginia Rail (*Rallus limicola*). Accidental in fall.

Sora (*Porzana carolina*). Occasional from spring to fall.

Black Rail (*Laterallus jamaicensis*). Accidental in summer.

American Coot (*Fulica americana*). Uncommon from spring to fall, breeding in the Park.

Semipalmated Plover (*Charadrius semipalmatus*). Rare in spring and fall.

Killdeer (*Charadrius vociferus*). Common to occasional from spring to fall, breeding in the Park; rare in winter.

Black-bellied Plover (*Pluvialis squatarola*). Rare in spring and fall.

American Woodcock (*Philohela minor*). Accidental in spring.

Common Snipe (*Gallinago gallinago*). Common from spring to fall, breeding in the Park; rare in winter.

Long-billed Curlew (*Numenius americana*). Occasional from spring to fall.

Spotted Sandpiper (*Actitus macularia*). Common from spring to fall, breeding in the Park.

Willet (*Catoptrophorus semipalmatus*). Occasional in spring and fall, rare during summer.

Solitary Sandpiper (*Tringa solitaria*). Rare in spring and fall.

Greater Yellowlegs (*Tringa malanoleuca*). Occasional migrant from spring to fall.

Lesser Yellowlegs (*Tringa flavipes*). Occasional migrant from spring to fall.

Pectoral Sandpiper (*Calidris melanotos*). Rare fall migrant.

Sanderling (*Calidris alba*). Accidental spring and fall migrant.

Baird's Sandpiper (*Calidris bairdii*). Rare fall migrant.

Semipalmated Sandpiper (*Calidris pusilla*). Accidental spring migrant.

Least Sandpiper (*Calidris minutilla*). Occasional spring and fall migrant.

Western Sandpiper (*Calidris mauri*). Rare fall migrant.

Stilt Sandpiper (*Micropalama himantopus*). Rare spring migrant.

Long-billed Dowitcher (*Limnodromus scolopaceus*). Occasional spring and fall migrant.

Marbled Godwit (*Limosa fedoa*). Rare spring and fall migrant.

American Avocet (*Recurvirostra americana*). Occasional migrant from spring to fall.

Wilson's Phalarope (*Phalaropus tricolor*). Uncommon spring and fall migrant, occasional summer visitor.

Northern Phalarope (*Phalaropus lobatus*). Rare to occasional spring and fall migrant.

Parasitic Jaeger (*Stercorarius parasiticus*). Accidental in summer.

California Gull (*Larus californicus*). Common from spring to fall.
Ring-billed Gull (*Larus delawarensis*). Rare spring and fall migrant.
Franklin's Gull (*Larus pipixcan*). Occasional from spring to fall.
Bonaparte's Gull (*Larus philadelphia*). Occasional spring migrant.
Common Tern (*Sterna hirundo*). Rare fall migrant.
Caspian Tern (*Sterna caspia*). Rare spring and summer migrant.
Black Tern (*Chlidonias niger*). Rare from spring to fall.
Band-tailed Pigeon (*Columba fasciata*). Accidental in spring and summer.
Mourning Dove (*Zenaida macroura*). Occasional from spring to fall.
Black-billed Cuckoo (*Coccyzus erythropthalmus*). Accidental in fall.
Screech Owl (*Otus asio*). Rare throughout the year, possibly breeding in the Park.
Great Horned Owl (*Bubo virginianus*). Occasional throughout the year, probably breeding in the Park.
Pygmy Owl (*Glaucidium gnoma*). Rare throughout the year, probably breeding in the Park.
Burrowing Owl (*Speotyto cunicularia*) Rare from spring to fall, probably breeding in the Park.
Great Gray Owl (*Strix nebulosa*). Occasional throughout the year, locally breeding in the Park.
Long-eared Owl (*Asio otus*). Occasional from summer to fall, probably breeding in the Park.
Short-eared Owl (*Asio flammeus*). Occasional in summer and fall, rare in winter and spring.
Boreal Owl (*Aegolius funereus*). Accidental in summer and fall.
Saw-whet Owl (*Aegolius acadius*). Rare throughout the year, possibly breeding in the Park.
Common Nighthawk (*Chordeiles minor*). Common from spring to fall, breeding in the Park.
White-throated Swift (*Aeronautes saxatilis*). Accidental in summer.
Black-chinned Hummingbird (*Archilochus alexandri*). Rare in spring and summer.
Broad-tailed Hummingbird (*Selaphorus platycercus*). Occasional from spring to fall, possibly breeding in the Park.
Rufous Hummingbird (*Selasphorus rufus*). Occasional from spring to fall.

III

Calliope Hummingbird (*Stellula calliope*). Common from spring to fall, breeding in the Park.

Belted Kingfisher (*Megacerle alcyon*). Common from spring to fall, breeding in the Park; occasional in winter.

Red-headed Woodpecker (*Melanerpes erythrocephalus*). Accidental in summer.

Acorn Woodpecker (*Melanerpes formicivorus*). Accidental in summer.

Lewis' Woodpecker (*Asyndesmus lewis*). Occasional from spring to fall, possibly breeding in the Park.

Yellow-bellied Sapsucker (*Sphyrapicus varius*). Common from spring to fall, breeding in the Park.

Williamson's Sapsucker (*Sphyrapicus thyroideus*). Occasional in spring and summer, breeding in the Park; rare in fall.

Hairy Woodpecker (*Dendrocopus villosus*). Common throughout the year, breeding in the Park.

Downy Woodpecker (*Dendrocopus pubescens*). Common throughout the year, breeding in the Park.

White-headed Woodpecker (*Dendrocopus albolarvatus*). Accidental in fall.

Black-backed Three-toed Woodpecker (*Picoides arcticus*). Occasional in spring and summer, breeding in the Park; rare in fall.

Northern Three-toed Woodpecker (*Picoides tridactylus*). Occasional from spring to fall, breeding in the Park; rare in winter.

Eastern Kingbird (*Tyrannus tyrannus*). Occasional from spring to fall.

Western Kingbird (*Tyrannus verticalis*). Rare from spring to fall.

Say's Phoebe (*Sayornis saya*). Rare from spring to fall.

Willow Flycatcher (*Empidonax traillii*). Uncommon from spring to fall, breeding in the Park.

Least Flycatcher (*Emipidonax minimus*). Accidental in summer.

Hammond's Flycatcher (*Empidonax hammondii*). Occasional from spring to fall.

Dusky Flycatcher (*Empidonax oberholseri*). Common from spring to fall, probably breeding in the Park.

Western Wood Pewee (*Contopus sordidulus*). Common from spring to fall, probably breeding in the Park.

Olive-sided Flycatcher (*Nuttallornis borealis*). Common from spring to fall, probably breeding in the Park.

Horned Lark (*Eremophila alpestris*). Occasional throughout the year.

Violet-green Swallow (*Tachycineta thalassina*). Occasional in spring and summer, probably breeding in the Park.

Tree Swallow (*Iridoprocne bicolor*). Abundant from spring to fall, breeding in the Park.

Bank Swallow (*Riparia riparia*). Common in spring and summer, probably breeding in the Park.

Rough-winged Swallow (*Stelgidopteryx ruficollis*). Rare in spring and summer.

Barn Swallow (*Hirundo rusticola*). Common in spring and summer, breeding in the Park.

Cliff Swallow (*Petrochelidon pyrrhonota*). Abundant in spring and summer, breeding in the Park, common in the fall.

Gray Jay (*Perisoreus canadensis*). Common throughout the year, breeding in the Park.

Steller's Jay (*Cyanocitta stelleri*). Common throughout the year, breeding in the Park.

Black-billed Magpie (*Pica pica*). Common throughout the year, breeding in the Park.

Common Raven (*Corvus corax*). Common throughout the year, breeding in the Park.

Common Crow (*Corvus brachyrhynchus*). Occasional throughout the year.

Pinyon Jay (*Gymnorhinus cyanocephalus*). Rare in summer and fall.

Clark's Nutcracker (*Nucifraga columbiana*). Common throughout the year, breeding in the Park.

Black-capped Chickadee (*Parus atricapillus*). Common throughout the year, breeding in the Park.

Mountain Chickadee (*Parus gambeli*). Common throughout the year, breeding in the Park.

White-breasted Nuthatch (*Sitta carolinensis*). Common throughout the year, breeding in the Park.

Red-breasted Nuthatch (*Sitta canadensis*). Occasional throughout the year, probably breeding in the Park.

Brown Creeper (*Certhia familiaris*). Occasional throughout the year, probably breeding in the Park.

Dipper (*Cinclus mexicanus*). Common throughout the year, breeding in the Park.

House Wren (*Troglodytes aedon*). Uncommon from spring to fall, breeding in the Park.

Marsh Wren (*Cistothorus palustris*). Occasional from spring to fall.

Rock Wren (*Salpinctes obeoletus*). Occasional from spring to fall, probably breeding in the Park.

Mockingbird (*Mimus polyglottos*). Accidental in summer and fall.

Gray Catbird (*Dumatilla carolinensis*). Rare to occasional from spring to fall.

Sage Thrasher (*Oreoscoptes montanus*). Occasional in spring and summer.

American Robin (*Turdus migratorius*). Abundant from spring to fall, breeding in the Park; rare in winter.

Hermit Thrush (*Catharus guttatus*). Common in spring and summer, breeding in the Park; occasional in fall.

Swainson's Thrush (*Catharus ustulatus*). Common in spring and summer, breeding in the Park; occasional in fall.

Veery (*Catharus fuscescens*). Occasional from spring to fall, probably breeding in the Park.

Western Bluebird (*Sialia mexicana*). Rare in spring and fall.

Mountain Bluebird (*Sialia currucoides*). Common from spring to fall, breeding in the Park.

Townsend's Solitaire (*Myadestes townsendi*). Occasional throughout the year.

Blue-gray Gnatcatcher (*Polioptila caerulea*). Accidental in fall.

Golden-crowned Kinglet (*Regulus satrapa*). Occasional from spring to fall; rare in winter.

Ruby-crowned Kinglet (*Regulus calendula*). Common to occasional from spring to fall, breeding in the Park; rare in winter.

Water Pipit (*Anthus spinoletta*). Common from spring to fall, probably breeding in the Park; rare in winter.

Sprague's Pipit (*Anthus spragueii*). Rare in spring and fall.

Bohemian Waxwing (*Bombycilla garrulus*). Occasional in winter and spring.

Cedar Waxwing (*Bombycilla cedrorum*). Occasional throughout the year.

Northern Shrike (*Lanius excubitor*). Occasional from fall to spring.

Loggerhead Shrike (*Lanius ludovicianus*). Rare in spring and summer.

Starling (*Sturnus vulgaris*). Common throughout the year, breeding in the Park; occasional in winter.

Solitary Vireo (*Vireo solitarius*). Rare in summer and fall.

Red-eyed Vireo (*Vireo olivaceus*). Occasional in spring and fall.

Warbling Vireo (*Vireo gilvus*). Uncommon to abundant from spring to fall, breeding in the Park.

114

Prothonotary Warbler (*Protonotaria citrea*). Accidental in summer.

Tennessee Warbler (*Vermivora peregrina*). Rare in summer.

Orange-crowned Warbler (*Vermivora celata*). Occasional from spring to fall.

Nashville Warbler (*Vermivora ruficapilla*). Accidental in spring and fall.

Yellow Warbler (*Dendroica petechia*). Common to abundant from spring to fall, breeding in the Park.

Yellow-rumped Warbler (*Dendroica coronata*). Common to abundant from spring to fall, breeding in the Park.

Townsend's Warbler (*Dendroica townsendi*). Rare in summer and fall.

Blackburnian Warbler (*Dendroica fusca*). Accidental in summer.

Northern Waterthrush (*Seiurus noveboracensis*). Rare in spring and summer.

MacGillivray's Warbler (*Oporonis tolmei*). Common from spring to fall, breeding in the Park.

Common Yellowthroat (*Geothlypis trichas*). Common from spring to fall, breeding in the Park.

Yellow-breasted Chat (*Icteria virens*). Accidental in spring and summer.

Wilson's Warbler (*Wilsonia citrina*). Common from spring to fall, breeding in the Park.

American Redstart (*Setophaga ruticilla*). Occasional in spring and summer.

House Sparrow (*Passer domesticus*). Common throughout the year, breeding in the Park.

Bobolink. (*Dolichonyx oryzivorus*). Rare in spring and summer.

Western Meadowlark (*Sturnella neglecta*). Uncommon from spring to fall, breeding in the Park.

Yellow-headed Blackbird (*Xanthocephala xanthocephala*). Common from spring to fall, breeding in the Park.

Red-winged Blackbird (*Agelaius phoeniceus*). Common from spring to fall, breeding in the Park; rare in winter.

Orchard Oriole (*Icterus spurius*). Accidental in spring.

Northern (Bullock's) Oriole (*Icterus galbula*). Occasional from spring to fall.

Brewer's Blackbird (*Euphagus cyanocephalus*). Common to abundant from spring to fall, breeding in the Park; rare in winter.

Brown-headed Cowbird (*Molothrus ater*). Common spring to fall, breeding in the Park.

Western Tanager (*Piranga ludovicianus*). Common from spring to fall, breeding in the Park.

Rose-breasted Grosbeak (*Pheuticus ludovicianus*). Occasional in spring, accidental in summer.

Black-headed Grosbeak (*Pheuticus melanocephalus*). Common to rare from spring to fall.

Indigo Bunting (*Passerina cyanea*). Accidental in spring and summer.

Lazuli Bunting (*Passerina amoena*). Occasional to rare from spring to fall, probably breeding in the Park.

Evening Grosbeak (*Hesperiphona vespertina*). Uncommon to occasional throughout the year.

Cassin's Finch (*Carpodacus cassinii*). Common from spring to fall, breeding in the Park; rare in winter.

House Finch (*Carpodacus mexicana*). Accidental from spring to fall.

Pine Grosbeak (*Pinicola enucleator*). Occasional throughout the year.

Gray-crowned Rosy Finch (*Leucosticte tephrocotis*). Common to rare throughout the year.

Black Rosy Finch (*Leucosticte atrata*). Common to occasional throughout the year, breeding in the Park.

Common Redpoll (*Acanthis flammea*). Rare in spring and fall.

Pine Siskin (*Spinus pinus*). Common from spring to fall, breeding in the Park; occasional in winter.

American Goldfinch (*Spinus tristis*). Occasional from spring to fall.

Red Crossbill (*Loxia curvirostra*). Occasional throughout the year, probably breeding in the Park.

White-winged Crossbill (*Loxia leucoptera*). Accidental in spring.

Green-tailed Towhee (*Chlorura chlorura*). Common to occasional from spring to fall, breeding in the Park.

Lark Bunting (*Calamospiza melanocorys*). Rare in spring and summer.

Savannah Sparrow (*Passerculus sandwichensis*). Common from spring to fall, breeding in the Park.

Vesper Sparrow (*Pooecetes gramineus*). Common from spring to fall, breeding in the Park.

Lark Sparrow (*Chondestes grammicus*). Occasional in summer and fall.

Black-throated Sparrow (*Amphispiza bilineata*). Accidental in spring.

Sage Sparrow (*Amphispiza belli*). Accidental in summer.

Dark-eyed (Oregon) Junco (*Junco hyemalis oreganus*). Common to abundant from spring to fall, breeding in the Park; occasional in winter.

Tree Sparrow (*Spizella arborea*). Occasional from fall to spring.

Chipping Sparrow (*Spizella passerina*). Common from spring to fall, breeding in the Park.

Clay-colored Sparrow (*Spizella pallida*). Rare in summer.

Brewer's Sparrow (*Spizella breweri*). Common from spring to fall, breeding in the Park.

Harris' Sparrow (*Zonotrichia querula*). Rare from fall to spring.

White-crowned Sparrow (*Zonotrichia leucophrys*). Abundant from spring to fall, breeding in the Park; rare in winter.

White-throated Sparrow (*Zonotrichia albicollis*). Rare fall migrant.

Fox Sparrow (*Passerella iliaca*). Occasional in spring and summer.

Lincoln Sparrow (*Melospiza melodia*). Common from spring to fall, breeding in the Park.

Swamp Sparrow (*Melospiza georgiana*). Accidental in fall.

Song Sparrow (*Melospiza melodia*). Common from spring to fall, breeding in the Park; occasional in winter.

McCown's Longspur (*Rhynchophanes mccownii*). Accidental in summer.

Lapland Longspur (*Calcarius lapponicus*). Accidental in spring.

Snow Bunting (*Plectrophenax nivalis*). Rare to occasional in fall and winter.

(*Additions to this list should be sent to the author or the Wyoming Game & Fish Department, 260 Buena Vista, Lander, Wyoming, in care of Nongame Bird Biologist*)

Mammals*

Masked Shrew (*Sorex cinereus*). Common

Vagrant Shrew (*Sorex vagrans*). Common

Dwarf Shrew (*Sorex nanus*). Rare

Northern Water Shrew (*Sorex palustris*). Uncommon

Little Brown Myotis (*Myotis lucifugus*). Common

Long-eared Myotis (*Myotis evotis*). Uncommon

Long-legged Myotis (*Myotis volans*). Uncommon

Silver-haired Bat (*Lasionycteris noctivagans*). Rare

Hoary Bat (*Lasiurus cinereus*). Rare

Pika (*Ochotona princeps*). Common

Showshoe Hare (*Lepus americanus*). Common

White-tailed Jackrabbit (*Lepus townsendii*). Uncommon

*Based on *Birds and Mammals of Grand Teton National Park*, published by the Grand Teton Natural History Association and the National Park Service.

Least Chipmunk (*Eutamias minimus*). Common
Yellow Pine Chipmunk (*Eutamias amoenus*). Common
Uinta Chipmunk (*Eutamias umbrinus*). Uncommon
Yellow-bellied Marmot (*Marmota flaviventris*). Common
Uinta Ground Squirrel (*Citellus armatus*). Abundant
Golden-mantled Ground Squirrel (*Citellus lateralis*). Common
Red Squirrel (*Tamiasciurus hudsonicus*). Abundant
Northern Flying Squirrel (*Glaucomys sabrinus*). Uncommon
Northern Pocket Gopher (*Thomomys talpoides*). Abundant
Beaver (*Castor canadensis*). Abundant
Deer Mouse (*Peromyscus maniculatus*). Abundant
Bushy-tailed Woodrat (*Neotoma cinerea*). Uncommon
Boreal Redback Vole (*Clethrionomys gapperi*). Common
Mountain Phenacomys (*Phenacomys intermedius*). Common
Richardson Vole (*Microtus richardsoni*). Common
Meadow Vole (*Microtus pennsylvanicus*). Abundant
Mountain Vole (*Microtus montanus*). Abundant
Long-tailed Vole (*Microtus longicaudus*). Uncommon
Sagebrush Vole (*Lagurus curtatus*). Rare
Muskrat (*Ondatra zibethicus*). Common
Western Jumping Mouse (*Zapus princeps*). Common
Porcupine (*Erethizon dorsatum*). Common
Coyote (*Canis latrans*). Abundant
Gray Wolf (*Canus lupus*). Extirpated
Red Fox (*Vulpes fulva*). Rare
Black Bear (*Ursus americanus*). Common
Grizzly Bear (*Ursus horribilis*). Rare
Marten (*Martes americana*). Common
Short-tailed Weasel (*Mustela erminea*). Uncommon
Long-tailed Weasel (*Mustela frenata*). Common
Mink (*Mustela vison*). Uncommon
Wolverine (*Gulo luscus*). Rare
Badger (*Taxidea taxus*). Common
Striped Skunk (*Mephitis mephitis*). Uncommon
River Otter (*Lutra canadensis*). Uncommon
Mountain Lion (*Felis concolor*). Rare
Lynx (*Lynx canadensis*). Rare

Bobcat (*Lynx rufus*). Rare
Elk (*Cervus canadensis*). Abundant
Mule Deer (*Odocoileus hemionus*). Common
Moose (*Alces alces*). Abundant
Pronghorn (*Antilocapra americana*). Uncommon
Bison (*Bison bison*). Uncommon
Bighorn Sheep (*Ovis canadensis*). Uncommon

Reptiles and Amphibians
Rubber Boa (*Charina bottae*). Rare
Western Garter Snake (*Thamnophis elegans*). Common
Common Garter Snake (*Thamophis sirtalis*). Common
Bull Snake (*Pituophis catenifer*). Rare
Tiger Salamander (*Ambystoma tigrinum*). Common
Western Toad (*Bufo boreas*). Common
Western Chorus Frog (*Pseudacris triseriata*). Common
Western Spotted Frog (*Rana pretiosa*). Common
Leopard Frog (*Rana pipiens*). Uncommon

Fishes
Mountain Whitefish (*Prosopium williamsoni*). Abundant
Brown Trout (*Salmo trutta*). Introduced, uncommon.
Cutthroat Trout (*Salmo clarki*). Abundant
Rainbow Trout (*Salmo gairdneri*). Introduced, uncommon.
Brook Trout (*Salvelinus fontinalis*). Introduced, common.
Lake Trout (*Salvelinus namaycush*). Introduced, common.
Utah Chub (*Gila atraria*). Abundant
Flathead Chub (*Hybopsis gracilis*). Introduced, rare.
Longnose Dace (*Rhinichthys cataractae*). Common
Speckled Dace (*Rhinichthys osculus*). Common
Redside Shiner (*Richardsonius balteatus*). Abundant
Leatherside Chub (*Snyderichthys copei*). Rare
Utah Sucker (*Catostomus ardens*). Abundant
Mountain Sucker (*Catstomus platyrhynchus*). Common
Mottled Sculpin (*Cottus bairdi*). Common
Piute Sculpin (*Cottus beldingi*). Common

List of Plants Mentioned in the Text*

Alder (*Alnus incana*)
Avalanche Lily (*Erythronium grandiflorum*)
Balsamroot (*Balsamorhiza sagittata*)
Big Sagebrush (*Artemisia tridentata*)
Bulrush (*Scirpus acutus*)
Caltha (*Caltha leptosepala*)
Colorado Blue Spruce (*Picea pungens*)
Cottonwood (*Populus angustifolia*)
Douglas Fir (*Pseudotsuga menziesii*)
Engelmann Spruce (*Picea engelmannii*)
Gilia (*Ipomopsis aggegata*)
Indian Paintbrush (*Castilleja* spp.)
Lodgepole Pine (*Pinus contorta*)
Menziesia (*Menziesia ferruginea*)
Mountain Ash (*Sorbus scopulina*)
Pondweed (*Potamogeton* spp).
Quaking Aspen (*Populus tremuloides*)
Rabbitbrush (*Chrysothamnus nauseosus*)
Rush (*Juncus* spp.)
Sedge (*Carex* spp.)
Spatterdock (*Nuphar polysepalum*)
Springbeauty (*Claytonia lanceolata*)
Subalpine Fir (*Abies lasiocarpa*)
Thimbleberry (*Rubus parviflorus*)
Watercrowfoot (*Batrachium trichophyllum*)
Whitebark Pine (*Pinus albicaulis*)
Willow (*Salix* spp.)

---

*Chapter opening ornaments for *Teton Wildlife* were drawn by Carolyn Ensle of the University of Colorado Herbarium, and correspond to this list as follows: 1. INTRODUCTION: Indian Paintbrush; 2. THE VALLEY OF THE GROS VENTRE: Douglas Fir Cone; 3. THE SAGEBRUSH SEA: Big Sagebrush; 4. THE WILLOW FLATS: Planeleaf Willow; 5. CHRISTIAN POND: Watercrowfoot; 6. THE OXBOW: Gilia; 7. THE ASPEN ISLAND: Quaking Aspen; 8. THE SPRUCE FOREST: Colorado Blue Spruce Cone; 9. THE CIRQUE: Avalanche Lily; 10. THE END OF SUMMER: Thimbleberry.

Sources and Bibliographic Notes

INTRODUCTION. Most of the information in this chapter is based on the booklet "Creation of the Teton Landscape," by J. D. Love and J. C. Reed, Jr., 1971, published by the Grand Teton Natural History Association, Moose, Wyoming. Another useful reference is *The Tetons, Interpretations of a Mountain Landscape*, by F. M. Fryxell, University of California Press, Berkeley, 1938. A recent pictorial approach is *The Grand Tetons*, by B. Norton, published by Viking Press, New York, 1974. A history of early man is presented in G. C. Fison's "Prehistoric Occupations of the Grand Teton National Park," *Naturalist* 22(1):35-37, 1971.

Of related interest are several publications available from the Wyoming Geological Survey, University of Wyoming, Laramie, including *Bulletin* 55, "Traveler's Guide to the Geology of Wyoming"; *Bulletin* 51, "A Field Guide to the Rocks and Minerals of Wyoming"; and *Bulletin* 54, "Fossils of Wyoming."

Finally, an excellent recent history of the Teton area is *Along the Ramparts of the Tetons, The Saga of Jackson Hole, Wyoming*, by Robert B. Betts, Colorado Associated University Press, 1978. The "flavor" of the area is also effectively captured in *Jackson Hole*, by Frank Calkins, Alfred A. Knopf, 1973.

THE VALLEY OF THE GROS VENTRE. The classic reference on the plant communities of Wyoming is "Life Zone Investigations in Wyoming," by M. Cary, Bureau of Biological Survey (now U.S. Fish and Wildlife Service), *North American Fauna* No. 42, 1917. More specifically for the Tetons is J. F. Reed's "The Vegetation of the Jackson Hole Wildlife Park, Wyoming," *American Midland Naturalist* 48: 700-729, 1952, which lists plants for the Snake River Oxbow. The ecology of the forested areas is discussed in L. Loope's "Dynamics of Forest Communities in Grand Teton National Park," *Naturalist* 22(1):39-47, 1971. Another ecological study is "A Synecological Study of the Forested Moraines of the Valley Floor of Grand Teton National Park, Wyoming," Ph.D. dissertation, 1966, Montana State University, Bozeman, by E. T. Oswold.

The birds of Grand Teton National Park were reviewed by D. B. Houston in "The Bird Fauna of Grand Teton National Park," Special Study No. 1, 14 pp. mimeo (copy in National Park Headquarters, Moose). A good published paper is by G. W. Salt, "An Analysis of Avifauna in the Teton Mountains and Jackson Hole, Wyoming," *Condor* 59:373-93, 1957. A check list of birds and mammals in the Park has been published by the Grand Teton Natural History Association, and a bird list is available from the Wyoming Game and Fish Department.

The classic study of elk is *The Elk of North America*, by O. J. Murie, Stackpole, 1951. Major technical references for Jackson Hole are: "The Elk of Jackson Hole: A Review of Jackson Hole Elk Studies," by C. C. Anderson, *Wyoming Game and Fish Commission Bulletin* 10, 158 pp, 1958, and "The Elk of Grand Teton and Southern Yellowstone National Parks," by G. F. Cole, National Park Service Research Report GRTE-N-1 (reissue), 80 pp. The most recent popular summary of elk biology in Jackson Hole is *Season of the Elk*, by Dean Krakel II, National Cowboy Hall of Fame and Western Heritage Center, 1975.

THE SAGEBRUSH SEA. The ecology of sagebrush in Wyoming has been discussed by A. A. Beetle in "A Study of Sagebrush," *Wyoming Agricultural Experiment Station Bulletin* 368, 1960, and its ecology in the park is covered in "Variation Within the Sagebrush Vegetation of Grand Teton National Park," by D. W. Sabinske and D. H. Knight, *Northwest Science* 52(3):195-204, 1978. A summary of the ecological relationships of sagebrush to nesting birds can be found in *Wilson Bulletin* 88:165-171, 1976.

There is a large amount of literature on the ecology and behavior of coyotes, including several recent books. Especially relevant to Wyoming is the study by Adolph Murie, "Ecology of the Coyote in the Yellowstone," U.S. National Park Service, *Fauna Series* No. 4, 1940, and O. J. Murie's "Food Habits of the Coyote in Jackson Hole, Wyoming," *U.S. Department of Agriculture Circular* No. 362, 1935. Most of my description of coyote whelping behavior is based on C. J. Snow's "Some Observations on the Behavioral and Morphological Development of Coyote Pups," *American Zoologist* 14 353-55, 1967, and M. Beckoff's "Social Play and Play-Soliciting in Infant Canids," *American Zoologist* 14:323-340, 1967. I have also used H. Silver and W. T. Silver, "Growth and Behavior of the Coyote-like Canid of New England . . ." *Wildlife Monographs* 17, 1969. Coyote behavior and ecology on the National Elk Refuge is described by

Franz Camenzind in a chapter of *Coyotes: Biology, Behavior and Management,* edited by Mark Beckoff. John Weaver describes coyote food habits in Grand Teton National Park and on the National Elk Refuge in "Coyote-Food Base Relationships in Jackson Hole, Wyoming," M.S. thesis, Utah State University, Logan, 88 pp, 1977.

Sources of information on pronghorn behavior primarily include D. W. Kitchen's "Social Behavior and Ecology of the Pronghorn," *Wildlife Monographs* 38, 1974, and R. E. Autenrieth and E. Fichter's "On the Behavior and Socialization of Pronghorn Fawns." *Wildlife Monographs* 42, 1975. Of related interest are "The Antelope of Colorado," *Colorado Department of Fish and Game Technical Bulletin* No. 4, 1959, and "Some Behavior Patterns of the Pronghorn," *Colorado Department of Game, Fish and Parks Special Report* No. 17, 1968.

THE WILLOW FLATS. The ecological relationships between moose and willows in Jackson Hole is documented in D. B. Houston's "The Shiras Moose in Jackson Hole, Wyoming," *Grand Teton Natural History Association Technical Bulletin* No. 1, 1968.

Although there are no comparable studies for Jackson Hole, the breeding biology of the greater sandhill crane has been documented at Grays Lake by R. C. Drewien's "Ecology of Rocky Mountain Greater Sandhill Cranes," Ph.D. dissertation, 1973, University of Idaho. The account of the crane attacking the moose is based on a note by M. Altmann (1960, *Journal of Mammalogy* 41:525), but the observations of the nest at the time of hatching are my own. The description of plumage and behavior development in young cranes is largely derived from L. M. Walkinshaw's "The Sandhill Cranes." *Cranbrook Institute of Science Bulletin* 29, 1949.

CHRISTIAN POND. Most of the observations on nesting trumpeter swans and associated species are my own. A separate account of trumpeter swans in the Tetons has also been published in *Natural History* (November 1978, pp. 72–77). A useful report on the breeding biology of trumpeter swans is that of R. D. Page, "The Ecology of the Trumpeter Swan on Red Rock Lakes National Wildlife Refuge, Montana," Ph.D. dissertation, 1974, University of Montana, Missoula. This work updates the original studies on this species by W. E. Banko "The Trumpeter Swan," U.S. Fish and Wildlife Service, *North American Fauna* 63,

1960. A history of the trumpeter swan in Wyoming appeared in *Wyoming Wildlife* 22(1): 8-14, 1958.

Details of the breeding biology of the common snipe can be found in L. M. Tuck's "The Snipes," *Canadian Wildlife Service Monograph Series* No. 5, 1972. Information on the white-crowned sparrow was from "Life Histories of North American Cardinals, Grosbeaks, Buntings, Towhees, Finches, Sparrows and Allies," *U.S. National Museum Bulletin* 237, 1968, edited by O. L. Austin, Jr.

THE OXBOW. Nearly all the information on the breeding behavior of the bald eagles is based on F. H. Herrick's *The American Eagle*, D. Appleton-Century Co., New York, 1934. Summaries of the status of this species in Wyoming appeared in *Wyoming Wildlife* 35(9):8-13, 1971, and in *Defenders of Wildlife* 43(2):148-52, 1968. There is also a recent study in Yellowstone Park by J. E. Swenson, "Ecology of the Bald Eagle and Osprey in Yellowstone National Park," M.S. thesis, 1975, Montana State University, Bozeman. Most of the information on osprey nesting is based on R. Green's "Breeding Behaviour of Ospreys *Pandion haliaetus* in Scotland," *Ibis* 118:475-90, 1976. Three references on great blue herons were especially useful: H. M. Pratt's "Breeding Biology of Great Blue Herons and Common Egrets in Central California," *Condor* 72:407-16, 1970, W. P. Cottrille and B. D. Cottrille's "Great Blue Heron: Behavior at the Nest," *University of Michigan Museum of Zoology Miscellaneous Publications* No. 102, 1958, and D. M. Mock's "Pair-formation Displays of the Great Blue Heron," *Wilson Bulletin* 88:185-230, 1976.

THE ASPEN ISLAND. The ecology of aspens in Jackson Hole, Wyoming, is described by A. A. Beetle, "Range Survey in Teton County, Wyoming, Part IV. Quaking Aspen," *Agricultural Experiment Station Publication* SM 27, March 1974, and in "Relationships among Aspen, Fire and Ungulate Browsing in Jackson Hole Wyoming," U.S. Forest Service and National Park Service, 33 pp, 1974, by G. Gruell and L. Loope.

Much of the information on common ravens is based on J. L. Dorn's "The Common Raven in Jackson Hole, Wyoming," M.S. thesis, 1972, University of Wyoming, Laramie. However, the account of ravens stealing eggs and young from herons is from my own observations, as was the earlier description of a raven attack on a trumpeter swan nest.

The account of elk calving and calf behavior is based on two studies by M. Altmann, "Social Behavior of Elk, *Cervus canadensis nelsoni*, in the Jackson Hole area of Wyoming," *Behaviour* 4:116-43, 1952, and "Patterns of Herd Behavior in Free-ranging Elk of Wyoming, *Cervus canadensis nelsoni*," *Zoologica* 41:65-71, 1956.

The behavior and biology of the prairie falcon is partly based on H. H. Enderson's "A Study of the Prairie Falcon in the Central Rocky Mountain Region," *Auk* 81:332-52, 1964, supplemented by my own observations. These include the description of the attack on the raven.

THE SPRUCE FOREST. The drumming log described at the start of this chapter is located near the cabin of Mrs. Mardy Murie, and the pine marten den was near one of the buildings occupied by Robert and Inger Koedt. One of the few studies of pine martens in the area is that of Adolph Murie, "Some Food Habits of the Marten," *Journal of Mammalogy* 42: 516-21, 1961. A more general study on this species in the Rocky Mountains is W. H. Marshall's "The Biology and Management of the Pine Marten in Idaho," Ph.D. dissertation, 1942, University of Michigan, Ann Arbor.

Most information on beavers in Jackson Hole comes from T. C. Collins's "Population Characteristics and Habitat Relations of Beavers, *Castor canadensis*, in Northwest Wyoming," Ph.D. dissertation, University of Wyoming, Laramie, 1976. W. Ruderstorf's "The Coactions of Beaver and Moose on a Joint Food Supply in the Buffalo River Meadows and Surrounding Area in Jackson Hole, Wyoming," M.S. thesis, Utah State University, Logan, 1952, provides additional information.

The information on the calliope hummingbird is mostly my own, based on a nest found by Dr. Alita Pinter, supplemented by published descriptions of nest characteristics and nest-building behavior. The description of the behavior of the female during the rainstorm was provided by Dr. Pinter. The orientation of the male relative to the sun during aerial display is from my own observations, but has been observed in at least one other species (*Wilson Bulletin* 77:38-44, 1965).

THE CIRQUE. The two primary references for the dipper were H. W. Hann's "Nesting Behavior of the American Dipper in Colorado," *Condor* 52:49–62,

1950, and G. J. Bakus's "Observations on the Life History of the Dipper in Montana," *Auk* 76:190-207, 1959.

The description of pika behavior is mostly derived from H. E. Broadbooks's "Ecology and Distribution of the Pikas of Washington and Alaska," *American Midland Naturalist* 73:299-335, 1965. Two related studies are H. R. Krear's "An Ecological and Ethological Study of the Pika (*Ochotona princeps* Bangs) in the Front Range of Colorado," Ph.D. dissertation, 1965, University of Colorado, Boulder, and J. H. Sevaraid's "The Natural History of the Pika (mammalian genus *Ochotona*)," Ph.D. dissertation, 1955, University of California, Berkeley.

The account of the mountain sheep is based on information in V. Geist's *Mountain Sheep*, University of Chicago Press, Chicago, 1971. Of related interest are "A Wyoming Bighorn Sheep Study," *Wyoming Fish and Game Department Bulletin* 1, 1942, and the paper by J. L. Oldemeyer et al., "Winter Ecology of Bighorn Sheep in Yellowstone National Park," *Journal of Wildlife Management* 35:257-69, 1971.

The account of black rosy finch nesting is derived from N. R. French's "Life History of the Black Rosy Finch," *Auk* 76:159-80, 1959.

THE END OF SUMMER. The description of beaver activities is mostly based on L. Trevis's "Summer Behavior of a Family of Beavers in New York State," *Journal of Mammalogy* 31:40-65, 1950. Information on the pine marten family is derived from J. D. Remington's "Food Habits, Growth, and Behavior of Two Captive Pine Martens," *Journal of Mammalogy* 33:66-70, 1952, and M. H. Markley and C. F. Bassett's "Habits of Captive Marten," *American Midland Naturalist* 28:604-16, 1942. The account of elk social behavior is based on the paper by M. Altmann mentioned earlier, and T. T. Struhsaker's "Behavior of Elk (*Cervus canadensis*) During the Rut," *Zeitschrift für Tierpsychologie* 24:80-114, 1967.

The check-list of vertebrates is based primarily on a list published by the Grand Teton Natural History Association and the U.S. National Service, with the names modified as necessary to bring them into current usage. A complete list of more than 900 species of vascular plants native to Grand Teton National Park, as well as keys and drawings to aid in their identification, is R. J. Shaw's *Field Guide to the Vascular Plants of Grand Teton National Park and Teton County, Wyoming*, Utah State University Press, Logan, 1976.